JOHN DENNIS:
THE OAKWELL YEARS

To Christopher,
Best Wishes
John Dennis
April 28th, 2012

JOHN DENNIS:
THE OAKWELL YEARS

*'It was sometimes like
watching Brazil...'*

John Dennis
and Matthew Murray

Wharncliffe Books

First published in Great Britain in 2012
by Wharncliffe Books
an imprint of
Pen and Sword Books Ltd
47 Church Street
Barnsley
South Yorkshire S70 2AS

Copyright © John Dennis and Matthew Murray, 2012

ISBN 978 1 84884 847 4

A CIP record for this book is available from the British Library

Printed and bound in England
by CPI Group (UK) Ltd, Croydon, CR0 4YY

Typeset in Times New Roman by
CHIC MEDIA LTD

Pen & Sword Books Ltd incorporates the imprints of
Pen & Sword Aviation, Pen & Sword Family History, Pen & Sword Maritime,
Pen & Sword Military, Pen & Sword Discovery, Wharncliffe Local History,
Wharncliffe True Crime, Wharncliffe Transport, Pen & Sword Select,
Pen & Sword Military Classics, Leo Cooper, Remember When,
The Praetorian Press, Seaforth Publishing and Frontline Publishing

For a complete list of Pen and Sword titles please contact
Pen and Sword Books Limited
47 Church Street, Barnsley, South Yorkshire, S70 2AS, England
E-mail: enquiries@pen-and-sword.co.uk
Website: www.pen-and-sword.co.uk

Contents

Acknowledgements

O ver the years, my wife and daughters have regularly urged me to commit to words my memories of my time at Barnsley Football Club. Additionally, friends and acquaintances who have listened to my reminiscences have also said that there's a book in there somewhere. I had no great urge to do it because I did not want to appear arrogant in assuming that people would be interested in what I had to say. Neither was I sure how to go about the task. The impetus finally came after a conversation with my co-author, Matthew Murray, who expressed interest in helping me with such a project. So here it is – my memories and the factual account of some of the events that took place at Barnsley Football Club over many years. I hope that those who read the book will enjoy my view of these events. It was a privilege to be the chairman of my hometown football club – the club that I started supporting as a boy, and which I will continue to support until I draw my last breath.

I would like to take this opportunity to pay personal tribute to all of those colleagues who served with me at various times on the Boards of Directors at Barnsley Football Club. In my early days as a newly appointed director, the board comprised of Chairman Geoff Buckle, Vice-Chairman Arthur Raynor, Ralph Potter, Norman Moody, Gordon Pallister, Charlie Williams and Johnny Steele. Barry Taylor was appointed at the same time as myself and went on to succeed Arthur Raynor as Vice-Chairman, and the make-up of the board when I first became chairman was Ralph Potter, Barry Taylor, Chris Harrison and Mick Hayselden, with Stuart Manley, John Kelly, Ian Potter, Mick Hall and Malcolm Hanson also joining the board at various times over the years. All of these men, like me, were committed Barnsley supporters who, whilst enjoying the privilege of being directors of the club they loved, also worked tirelessly for the benefit of the club. Over the years, I was lucky to receive virtually wholehearted support and

ACKNOWLEDGEMENTS

encouragement as their colleague and chairman, and although we had our moments from time to time, I will remain eternally grateful to all of those men. The general manager/secretary of the Football Club throughout all of my time as a director and chairman was Michael Spinks, who was devoted to his job and was incredibly loyal. For Michael and for many others employed behind the scenes at Oakwell, working for the club wasn't just a job, it was a vocation. I would also like to pay tribute to Matthew Murray, my co-author, for providing the impetus to get me focused on this project and for his advice and guidance in putting this book together. I hope his health doesn't suffer too much from the ill effects of passive smoking and the large variety of cakes that we ate whilst completing this project.

Finally, I would like to say a sincere thank you to the many fans of Barnsley Football Club. Over the years, whilst getting my fair share of stick, most of which was probably deserved, I did also receive a great deal of support and inspiration from the wonderful Barnsley fans. To this day, I am regularly approached by fans wanting to talk about some of the great times and I'm always touched by the sincerity and kindness still shown to me.

John Dennis,
January 2012

Dedication

This book is dedicated to my beloved wife, Christianne, and our two wonderful daughters, Sarah and Caroline. Over the years, their love, understanding, patience and support have kept me going in good times and bad.

Introduction

Miracle at Oakwell

Neil Redfearn had the ball just outside the Bradford City box before slipping it through to the little man from Trinidad, Clint Marcelle. Clint jinked to the left, then the right, before stroking the ball past Bradford keeper Aidan Davison and into the net. We had done it – a 2-0 victory would secure top-flight status for the first time in the history of Barnsley Football Club.

The game had not been such plain sailing. Despite taking the lead through a Paul Wilkinson goal after about twenty minutes, the team hadn't been at its best that day and was perhaps a little nervous, feeling the pressure of such a huge match. Wilko assures me he meant to guide his header perfectly into the far corner, but I'm convinced it went in off his shoulder. But who really cares? We were 1-0 up and heading for Premier League glory. I thought the goal might settle us, but it didn't. Bradford, who themselves needed points in their battle against relegation, hit the post and went close on a number of other occasions. Prior to kick-off I had been confident that we would gain the three points needed to achieve our ambition – a confidence that was quite unusual for a lifelong Barnsley supporter. Late in the second half with five minutes remaining, Marcelle was fed that all-important through ball by Redfearn, and when he slotted the ball passed the goalkeeper we all knew that the script had been written and promotion was ours. We were about to hit the big time! When the final whistle sounded, mayhem ensued as thousands of ecstatic Barnsley fans swarmed onto the pitch. People young and old flooded the playing surface that afternoon to mob their heroes and take joy in the fact that Danny

Wilson's men had gained promotion to the Premier League. The now famous 'It's just like watching Brazil' song could be heard for miles around as Barnsley Football Club, its players, its staff and its supporters tried to take in the enormity of what had just been achieved.

As the sea of people flocked onto the pitch to celebrate on that nerve-wracking Saturday afternoon of 26 April 1997, I, John Dennis, the Chairman of Barnsley Football Club, felt a maelstrom of emotions, unconfined joy, enormous pride and great happiness for everybody at the club and its supporters who were revelling in this moment. But as the celebrations got underway, I needed to take a moment to reflect on what had happened. Hugs and kisses were exchanged with my wife and daughters, as well as with my fellow directors – not the kisses! – and I stepped across from the directors' box and into the now empty visiting directors' section. With a tear in my eye, I looked on at the joyous scenes unfolding in front of me. Years of toil, hard work and many ups and downs flashed before my eyes. I couldn't help but think of my late father, Ernest, who had previously been the chairman of Barnsley Football Club and who had put much time and effort into the club, as well as investing his own money at one time to save the Reds from going out of business. I hoped, wherever he was, that he was looking on at these scenes. He would have been so proud to see what his beloved Barnsley had achieved that day. I felt a hand on my shoulder and glanced behind me to see Oakwell legend, Johnny Steele, who had occupied many roles at the club spanning seven decades, including player, manager, youth team coach, reserve team coach, secretary, general manager, director and now vice-president. With tears in his eyes and a quiver in his voice, he said: "I know who you're thinking about now. He would have been so proud." It was a very moving moment because Johnny and my father had been very close. As a young man I used to hear the two of them on the phone to each other as they spent hours discussing Football Club business. After that brief reflective moment I resumed my duties as proud chairman, joining in with the rest of the Barnsley faithful in celebrating this historic achievement. The fans were in the mood to party – and so was I. Barnsley Football Club had deservedly made it into the Premier League.

But before the serious celebrations began, I had to take care of a few family matters because my wife had insisted I get Super Johnny Hendrie's shirt so she could keep it as a souvenir. Also, my youngest daughter wanted Andy Liddell's shirt and my eldest girl asked for Dave Watson's goalkeeper's jersey. I had learnt the hard way that you should never argue with one woman, let alone three, so I made my way down to the dressing room and hunted down my targets. But first, of course, I sought out Danny, and gave him a huge bear hug before doing the same to Eric Winstanley and then the players. They repaid me by drenching me with champagne, which had been bought and placed strategically in various parts of the ground in preparation for the triumph. I was amazed that Hendrie, Liddell and Watson handed over their shirts without any arguments, although being the club chairman gives you a certain amount of clout.

Having had a few minutes with the lads, I then spent an age talking to the local and national press before going to the boardroom to celebrate with my colleagues. Our guests from Bradford City, who must have been hurting after this defeat had put a dent in their survival hopes, seemed genuinely delighted for us and I must pay tribute to the way that Geoffrey Richmond and his colleagues behaved that day. Their supporters, of course, were equally as magnanimous in sharing the joy of their Barnsley counterparts, and it was a wonderful gesture by a number of Reds fans when they went to support City the following week as they won their survival battle with a victory over Charlton Athletic. By the time I got back to the boardroom we had run out of champagne glasses (but not champagne), so I was obliged to drink mine out of half pint glasses. After a couple of hours, my colleagues and our families moved across to the East Stand hospitality area where the celebrations continued with renewed vigour as we shared the joy of the occasion with box holders and executive members. As the night wore on, we were told that there was 'one hell of a party' taking place in town, so we decided we'd join in. We took taxis up to Wellington Street, where there was indeed one hell of a party. We stumbled into the Theatre Bar to join in the celebrations and, needless to say, I didn't have to buy a drink all night. As the evening started to wind down the bar's owner, Barry Smith, very sensibly arranged transport for us, and I have a vague memory of being led gently away.

Winning promotion to the Premier League was obviously the proudest moment in my time as chairman. There have been other ups and many downs, lots of wheeling and dealing and much joy and stress. A few of the stories can never be printed, but many of them can, and I hope you enjoy the journey as I give you a different perspective of our beloved Barnsley Football Club and the truth behind the headlines.

CHAPTER 1

Fruity Beginnings

I have no idea why my mother decided to give birth to me in Sheffield, but on 6 September 1950, at Jessop's Hospital, John Dennis entered the world. The fact that I was born in Sheffield is a slight blot on my otherwise perfect Barnsley CV, but I hope Reds' fans can forgive me because I was only in Sheffield for a few days before returning to the family home on Dodworth Road, Barnsley. Born to Mr Ernest Dennis and Mrs Jean Dennis, I'm told I lived at that address for seven months before the family moved to 4 Victoria Street. We stayed there from 1951 until 1961, our next move taking us to 15 Granville Street, just off Huddersfield Road.

I was very fortunate to have had a comfortable upbringing, although I didn't see much of my father because he would be up for work and be gone before breakfast to run the family wholesale fruit and vegetable business, A Dennis Limited, and wouldn't get home until early evening. My father wasn't the most approachable of people and it wasn't until I started working for him, in my late teens that I developed a strong relationship with him. Nonetheless, I always knew that he was proud of myself and my brother Anthony. The image that the world saw of him was a bluff, gruff Yorkshireman with a tough exterior, but underneath he could be a very gentle and kindhearted man. Mother, on the other hand, was a total contrast, tending to wear her heart on her sleeve. She was organised, house proud, a great cook and a very elegant woman who wouldn't dream of going out, even to go shopping, without her full make-up on and being smartly dressed. She was a very capable woman who dedicated herself to her family,

1

although when she was in her late forties she demonstrated just how capable she was by being appointed as a magistrate in the town and becoming one of the most respected of her peers. My parents met before the war when my mother worked as a beautician at Walsh's Department Store in Sheffield. They married in February 1947, at St Peter's Church on Doncaster Road, Barnsley, near to my grandparents' home at The Cedars, their wedding having been much delayed due to the war as my father didn't return from active service in Burma until early 1946.

You could say that it was destiny that I would be associated with Barnsley Football Club because on the day that I was born the Reds had a home match against Brentford, which, incidentally, was won 1-0. Many years later, for my fiftieth birthday, my fellow director, Mick Hayselden, presented me with an original framed matchday programme from that game, which hangs proudly in my study at home to this very day.

School for me started at Wilthorpe Nursery School and then St Matthew's Infant School on Summer Lane, before a one-year stint at St Mary's Boys' School on Churchfields, on the site of the current police station. Just a week after my ninth birthday I was packed off to boarding school in North Nottinghamshire, a school called Ranby House, near Retford, where I was to spend the next five years. Ranby was a rugby-playing school in the Christmas term, in the spring term we played hockey and in the summer we took to the cricket field. I played in most of the teams and was what you might describe as average, determined and enthusiastic, but not particularly gifted. By this stage in my life I was well into football, which unsurprisingly was frowned upon at my rugby-playing school. They didn't particularly like us playing casual football matches in our spare time, but I remember one occasion when we just couldn't resist. I would have been about twelve, it was the beginning of the Christmas term and we were desperate for a kick-about. The school boasted a beautiful grass tennis court, which was mainly used by the staff. The tennis season was over so the net had been taken down, and my mates and I thought it would be perfect for a game of five-a-side. We used this beautifully manicured tennis court for our footballing pleasures, and even I felt like Bobby Charlton as I effortlessly sprayed the ball to all corners of the park. Needless to say it was a short-lived pleasure because after about half an hour one of the teachers appeared and sent us all inside for a serious telling off. Unfortunately, the next eight Wednesday afternoons were spent in detention as punishment for our sins, but it was worth it just to play on that surface.

Most of my friends at school were football fans, many of whom supported Nottingham Forest and Leicester, but unfortunately there were a few Sheffield Wednesday followers too. Barnsley Football Club had become a real passion of mine after my father had introduced me to the Reds. He himself was a dedicated Barnsley fan, but additionally had played a major role in re-establishing the Supporters' Club in 1948. In those days there was a natural progression for senior officials of the Supporters' Club to seek nomination to the Board of Directors, and during the 1950s my father had enjoyed two spells as a director of the club. Whether he was on the board or not, though, he always bought three season tickets for Oakwell in what was then known as the Centre Stand, now the West Stand, on Row E seats 77, 78 and 79. Having tried and failed to indoctrinate my elder brother into Barnsley Football Club my father took me to my first game in the 1957-58 season for a friendly match against Arsenal. In those days if clubs got knocked out of the FA Cup in the early rounds, they would try and arrange friendly matches for any blank Saturdays, and this was one such match. My Barnsley-watching career had fairly inauspicious beginnings as Arsenal, playing in green shirts with white sleeves, hammered Barnsley 6-0. I also recall another match from that era when Barnsley took on a Representative XI from the local leagues. That match went a bit better, with Barnsley winning 12-1 in the sort of game that you would never see taking place these days.

In terms of serious football watching I first went to league games in the 1958-59 campaign, when the club was relegated from the old Second Division. The team was managed by Tim Ward and featured Harry Hough in goal, John Short and Colin Swift at full-back, Duncan Sharp at centre-half, Arthur Kaye on the right wing, John McCann on the left wing with Lol Chappell at centre forward. Malcolm Graham played inside left, Frank Bartlett was inside right and the wing halves were usually Bobby Wood and Billy Houghton. My first home league game was to see the Reds beat Grimsby Town 3-1, and I recall other home fixtures that season against Derby County, Rotherham United and Middlesbrough. My first away outing was on Boxing Day 1958, when my father gave the family a real Christmas treat by taking us all to Ayresome Park to watch Barnsley take on Middlesbrough. We lost 3-1 and played in a changed strip of blue shirts and white shorts. I also have vivid memories of going to Hillsborough for the last game of that season to watch us against our old rivals, Sheffield Wednesday. They were promoted that season and we were fighting relegation, so I guess it shouldn't have been such a big surprise that we got thrashed 5-0. Our best player that day was goalkeeper Don Leeson, who had replaced Harry Hough. Even at that age I didn't take defeat very well and wasn't much company for my father as we travelled back from Sheffield. Sadly, it was a feeling I'd come to experience a few more times later in life.

Football played a huge part in my childhood because, not only was my father a committed supporter, but my mother and grandfather were also devout fans. My grandfather, Arnold (whose name I unfortunately inherited as my middle one), used to take me to watch the reserve team games at Oakwell every other Saturday. Reserve team football was very different to what it is now because when the first team were away, the reserves would be at home, the purpose being for clubs to try to recreate, as nearly as possible, the competitive conditions of a normal matchday fixture. The teams weren't made up of a collection of youngsters and trialists with the odd pro thrown in – as they are these days – but were the next best XI that weren't on duty with the first team. Barnsley played in the Central League and along with Bury were the only two clubs that didn't feature in the top two divisions of the Football League. The Central League was a Midlands and North based league, so members of the League included the likes of Manchester United, Manchester City, Liverpool and Everton, Sheffield Wednesday and Sheffield United, Leeds and Burnley, the latter being a top club at that time. I particularly enjoyed seeing a star-studded Manchester United reserve team coming to Oakwell one afternoon and putting on the style as they slaughtered Barnsley 11-5. Going to reserve team matches with my grandfather was one of life's great pleasures for me at that time.

In the late 1950s and early 1960s there were very few highlights to treasure as a Barnsley supporter, other than a great cup run in season 1960-61. The run began on Bonfire Night 1960, with a not very promising 0-0 draw at Redheugh Park, the home of Gateshead Football Club. The replay four days later saw us dispatch our non-league opponents 2-0 at Oakwell. We travelled to Valley Parade in the second round, where two Frank Bartlett goals saw us home. Elm Park, Reading was the venue for our third round tie, where a Bert Tindill strike gave us a well deserved 1-1 draw. The replay took place on the Wednesday afternoon at Oakwell, and again the Reds were triumphant, this time 3-1 after extra time. The midweek afternoon kick-off is explained by the fact that, in those days, there were no floodlights at Oakwell. The fourth round gave us yet another away tie, at West Yorkshire rivals Huddersfield Town. Another 1-1 draw meant another replay at Oakwell, with the Reds winning 1-0 in front of a quite remarkable 29,000 crowd. The attendance was even bigger twelve days later when 33,000 packed into Oakwell as First Division Luton Town were dispatched 1-0. On 14 March we travelled to Filbert Street to face top flight Leicester City, and once again, the Reds battled through to another Oakwell replay, securing a 0-0 draw. An incredible 39,000 people crammed into Oakwell the following Wednesday afternoon, the majority of whom were to go home disappointed as Leicester edged the game 2-1 after extra time. They, of course, went on to lose in the final to a Danny Blanchflower-inspired Tottenham Hotspur as Spurs completed the double that season. From my own point of view it was bitterly disappointing that, because of my boarding school education, I was only able to see a solitary match in this run – the Reading replay – although I listened to live commentary of the Leicester replay on my transistor radio as I wandered around the rugby fields at school.

Football occasionally intruded into some of the Dennis family holidays. One particular year on the first day of the football season, we were holidaying near Arbroath and my father asked me if I fancied going to a game. I couldn't believe my luck as off we went to watch Arbroath versus Hamilton Academicals. Hamilton wore a red and white strip, similar to that worn by Barnsley, so I spent the afternoon willing them to win, which they did 4-0. My father and I sat on the Arbroath directors' bench, which was pitch side, with their board members and their manager. This caused some bizarre transfer rumours as my father was, at the time, a director of Barnsley. His visit sparked speculation in the local press that Barnsley were interested in signing Arbroath goalkeeper Bobby Williamson. It was absolute rubbish, although ironically Bobby did sign for Barnsley a couple of years later, but it had nothing to do with my father's initial visit. In the midweek it was the big local derby between Montrose and Arbroath, at Montrose, so we went to that as well. That game finished 2-2. The following year we were on the other side of Scotland, staying in Helensburgh. Desperate to see a game I trawled the local paper to see what football was on and there was nothing – until I started looking at the Reserve League fixtures. Much to my delight, I discovered that Dumbarton Reserves were at home to Queen of the South Reserves that particular day, so that's where we went, and I seem to remember that Queen of the South won 7-1.

At school I was quite a bright lad, doing well at Ranby House, gaining a £100 per year scholarship for Worksop College where I went aged fourteen. The fees for Worksop were £400 per year so the scholarship was a big help to my parents. Worksop College was a tough, traditional all-boys boarding school. Fortunately, I continued to do quite well academically, getting my O-level in Maths when I was fourteen, before picking up a further ten O-levels when I took them the following year. For my A-levels I studied English and French, as I'd always been reasonably good at languages, with my third subject being Politics and Economics. In the sixth form things became a little more relaxed and other pleasures manifested themselves, including the obvious traditional ones that sixteen-year-old indulge in. As education progressed, a debate was ongoing in our household about whether I should go into the family business or go to university. My father always had this picture of myself and my brother working alongside him at the firm. My brother had made it clear that he wanted to go into the business and for a number of years would spend his school holidays at work in the warehouse on Midland Street and going out with the delivery lorries. I had never really thought that was a great way of spending your holidays and I fondly remember many happy hours playing table football at the bowling alley next to the bus station in Barnsley, which is now the Gala Bingo building.

In those days you would fill out your UCCA (University Central Councils for Admission) forms and you had to put down your choice of universities. Bizarrely, football even had a say in these key decisions with my first choice being the University of Kent, as I really fancied seeing the Barnsley games in London and particularly Gillingham, where I'd never been. Choice number two was the University of Exeter so I could see the lads in the West Country at Exeter, Torquay and Plymouth. Options three and four were Sheffield and Hull so that I could get to all of the home games and, strangely, I seem to remember my fifth option was St Andrew's University in Scotland, because I had always been a closet East Fife supporter.

By the Easter holidays of 1968 I had to make a decision – university or the fruit business. I have to confess that I hadn't been quite as hardworking during sixth form as in my earlier school years, and I wasn't as confident as I might have been about getting the A-level grades that I needed. My father sat me down for a chat and I told him that what I'd really like to do was go and experience university for four years before joining the business. He, and let me paraphrase, replied: "If you think you're going to spend four years at university wasting my money then you've got another thing coming. Make a decision!" As it turned out my A-level results were disappointing so even though I got an offer from Strathclyde University under the clearing system, I had already made my mind up to go into the business. However, I was disappointed that I'd let myself down with a poor result in Politics and Economics, so I decided to go to Barnsley

7

Technical College, nowadays known as Barnsley College, to take evening classes with a view to re-sitting and passing the A-level. Sadly it didn't last long as one of my classes was at 6pm on a Wednesday evening – an hour before the new kick-off time for Barnsley Reserves' home games. I decided that Politics and Economics on a Wednesday evening was far less interesting than watching Barnsley Reserves, so each week I went through the charade of pretending to go to my class but instead headed off to Oakwell for the match. I had to be careful though because I didn't want the old man to see me. Fortunately, I don't think he did, or at least he never told me had done, although I guess the crafty old devil knew what was going on because my potential A-level qualification in Politics and Economics was never mentioned at home again.

I had actually left school on Monday 15 July 1968, and that evening my father asked me when I thought I'd be starting work. My response was that I would like a holiday somewhere and that some of the lads were talking about a trip around Europe, so I offered to join him some time in September. He replied: "That's very kind of you, but set your alarm for 5.30am next Monday morning because that's when you're starting." So, on Monday 22 July 1968, I started work at A Dennis Limited as a trainee salesman, which to cut through the euphemism, meant general dog's body and barrow boy. After public school, the early mornings, the long days and the rigours of the fruit trade were a real shock to the system and more than once in those early days, I wondered what I'd done. My father used to dish out some quite serious rollockings and I wasn't exempt. I had got into this rather cosy little habit of joining some of the other warehouse lads for a fry-up at the nearby bus station café, with a big mug of coffee, a cigarette and a read of the paper to round things off. I had been doing this for a couple of weeks, my absence from the business didn't seem to have been noticed and I was really getting quite accustomed to this little treat. However, this indulgence was about to come to a grinding halt because one particular morning I heard this almighty racket coming from the direction of our warehouse at the bottom of Midland Street and realised that my absence had finally been noticed. As I tried to sneak back into work, still wiping egg from my chin, I failed to escape the attention of my father who, in front of customers, staff and the general public walking past on the pavement, gave me one of the biggest rollockings I've ever had in my life. That was my last trip to the bus station café.

I had started work on a fiver a week, rather less than the other warehouse lads were paid. When I was eighteen, I was given a £1 pay rise and on my nineteenth birthday I was in for another shock pay adjustment. The company's Admin Manager Rita Fairhurst – a wonderful, hardworking woman who worked for my father, and then for me, for many years – told me that there was a nice little surprise for me in my pay packet and not to forget to thank my father when I saw him at lunchtime. On opening up my brown envelope I was pleasantly surprised to find I'd been given a £2 rise, which may not sound a lot these days but when beer was half a crown for a pint and cigarettes were three shillings for twenty the extra money would be quite handy. Over lunch I thanked my father for the pay rise, to which he replied: "I don't think you're paying your mother anything for board and lodgings. As your brother is paying her £2 per week, I think it's time you did the same." On returning to work I told Mrs Fairhurst what had happened, and she delivered a further blow when she explained that my £2 pay rise would take me into the threshold for national insurance and income tax so in fact, I'd be ten bob a week worse off. This was just one of many life-forming experiences working for Ernest Dennis in the wholesale fruit business in Barnsley.

CHAPTER 2

The Importance of Being Ernest

I t might not seem that unusual for Barnsley fans to hear, but in the mid 1960s the club was going through a very difficult period, both financially and on the pitch. Following relegation from the Second Division at the end of the 1958-59 season, my father had a brief spell back on the board but lost his seat in 1965 following the club's further relegation to Division Four. Times were dire and with crowds down to 2,500-3,000, Barnsley Football Club was in trouble. By the autumn of 1966, there were genuine fears that the club might fold as the team hit rock bottom in the Football League. My father took it upon himself to try and do something about it, canvassing various different businessmen in the town to ask if they would join with him in putting a few bob into the club. My father didn't have pots of money but he thought that if he could get a few like-minded people to follow his lead then he believed his beloved Barnsley Football Club could be saved. He eventually went to see a man named Frank Buckle, the father of my predecessor as chairman, Geoff Buckle. The Buckles operated a transport business called John Walker's, situated at the top of Cemetery Road. Frank said that the only person he could imagine who would be daft enough to invest in the Football Club would be his son Geoff, so a meeting was arranged. They agreed to make a small investment in the club, subject to certain proposals being accepted by the board. The chairman at the time was Sir Joseph Richards, who was then President of the Football League and a very influential football figure. Sir Joseph stood down as chairman with his place being taken by local businessman Sid Edmondson. Arthur Raynor, whose café in The Arcade was renowned for the quality of its pies, became vice-chairman with my father and Geoff joining the board as directors.

With the money that was injected, the club bought two new players, the first being Barry Thomas, a prolific goal scorer throughout his career with Mansfield Town, Scunthorpe United and Newcastle United. On leaving the Geordies he had re-signed for Scunthorpe and although he had a longstanding knee problem, Barnsley splashed out £7,500 for his signature. Johnny Evans, a much-travelled lower league inside forward who had always scored goals, joined Thomas at Oakwell from Exeter City for £2,500. With the impetus that was created by the signings of two new front men, manager Johnny Steele and the whole squad were invigorated and the team began to climb the table, finishing in sixteenth place – an achievement that had looked impossible in those early dark days of the season. The fans responded to this upturn in fortunes by returning to Oakwell in far greater numbers. Off the field the reshaped board received devastating news when very soon after being appointed as chairman, Mr Edmondson collapsed and died in December 1966. Vice-Chairman Arthur Raynor took over as acting chairman until the following summer, when at a sparsely attended board meeting my father was voted in as chairman. A number of the board were less than pleased with that outcome, viewing it as a ruthless pitch by my father for the chairman's role. It didn't exactly endear him to everyone on the board, but he believed he was the right man for the job and in that frame of mind, Ernest was not a man to argue with.

My father being chairman made little difference to my football watching. For home games I continued to sit on Row E in the old Centre Stand using the family season tickets, and would pay for my own tickets for away games. On the odd occasion my father treated me, most notably for an away League Cup tie at Highbury in 1971 when he invited me into the directors' box. Although we lost the game 1-0, it was a great experience to see behind the scenes at such a great club. One particular joy that I remember from those times was listening to my father talk to the manager, Johnny Steele, on his loudspeaker telephone for hours and hours about football in general and Barnsley Football Club in particular. When the old man had got the Football Club on the phone the fruit business was put on hold and it was fascinating to hear at first hand some of the day-to-day goings-on at Oakwell. My father was well connected in football circles and got me tickets for a number of FA Cup finals. I remember going to see West Brom versus Everton in 1968, Leeds versus Sunderland in 1973 and Arsenal versus Ipswich Town in 1978. On another occasion he offered me tickets for an FA Cup semi-final between Manchester United and Leeds at Hillsborough, but that same day Barnsley were taking on Millwall at Oakwell, so there was only one place I was going (we won 4-1). For the 1966 World Cup my father obtained two season tickets for all of the games due to be played at Wembley. England were based there for their group matches and he gave his tickets for those games to customers of the business. He and I went to the quarter-final game against Argentina and the semi-final against Portugal, but then he committed the unforgivable sin of taking my mother to the final against West Germany. I was really disappointed, and had to settle for watching the game at home on television. It is, of course, history that England won the World Cup that day and many years later, mine and many other people's memories were stirred one afternoon at Ardsley House at a fundraising lunch when Alan Ball, a member of the World Cup winning team, gave us a spellbinding account of what it was like to be one of eleven English born footballers to lift the game's greatest prize.

Throughout the twelve years of my father's chairmanship, life was a real struggle for Barnsley Football Club. There were one or two highlights, such as the Fourth Division promotion campaign of 1967-68 season. The club went into the penultimate game of that season away at Chester, needing a point to secure promotion. That day I was playing cricket for Worksop College 3rd XI (I said I was average) against a village cricket club called Wiseton, near Bawtry. At that time there were no mobile phones or speedy Internet services, so you had to rely on Sports Report to get the results. I remember waiting with baited breath as the results came through and when I heard that we had drawn 1-1, the cheer was probably heard back in Barnsley. For the record, the legendary Eric Winstanley scored for the Reds.

The celebrations didn't last long and things again got tough at Oakwell. Johnny Steele had stood down as manager in 1971 to be replaced by John McSeveney. At the end of season 1971-72 we were back in the Fourth Division, having needed a win at Port Vale on the last day of the season to survive. Following relegation McSeveney was replaced as manager by Johnny Steele, who was starting his second stint in the Oakwell hot seat. I was surprised that McSeveney had lasted that long because after a particularly horrendous 6-0 hammering at Oldham at the end of February, I returned home to Granville Street to find the house in complete darkness, but as I opened the door I heard voices. Fearing the worst, I crept inside only to discover my father and Geoff Buckle in deep discussion over a bottle of whiskey about the future of the manager. After that defeat at Port Vale, my father took the players into the old social club on their return from the Potteries to commiserate with them over a beer. Poor old John McSeveney must have had a pretty good idea of what was in store for him when having offered to buy my father a drink the reply was: "I'll buy my own so-and-so drinks, thank you very much." Relegation meant further financial pressures on the club and during this period my father agreed a deal to sell the Grove Street car park to Fine Fare Supermarkets for £250,000, subject to planning permission. It did not sound like a lot of money for such a sizeable plot to me and a couple of nights later I was in the pub with a pal of mine, Steve Wright, who was in the property business. I gave Steve brief details about the deal, which I really shouldn't have done, and Steve felt that the land should be worth a lot more than that. When I got home that night I told the old man about the conversation and he arranged to meet Steve at the old Barnsley Gentleman's Club, at the top of Regent Street. Following their discussions Steve found a client who was prepared to pay £400,000, subject to planning permission, with his client being willing to put down a ten per cent deposit. Those were desperate times for Barnsley Football Club and because the club was so strapped for cash, the deposit was used to pay day-to-day bills, which in hindsight wasn't a great idea. Inevitably, of course, the planning application was rejected and the club had six months to find the cash to repay the deposit. I had wondered what the old man was going to do and I was soon to find out. At that time the family business had recently relocated from our town centre site on Midland Street, just behind the bus station, to the old Corporation Cleansing Department premises on Pontefract Road. We had sold our building on Midland Street for £130,000 and having developed the new site still had substantial funds in the bank. Then, one horrible, cold Tuesday afternoon during February, my brother and I were sat behind our desks in the office we shared with our father when he said he had some news for us. It transpired that he had decided that the business was going to lend the Football Club the £40,000 it needed to repay the deposit on the land. I said: "Do you really think that's wise?" His reply was: "Probably not, but it's too late now because the money's already been transferred." He then left the office to go up to Oakwell and my brother asked me if I thought we'd ever get it back. "Not a dog's chance," was my response.

Thankfully I was made to eat my words when in 1976 the club sold two players for substantial transfer fees. The first of these players was full-back Martin Gorry, who went to Newcastle United for £50,000, and the second was Anton Otulakowski, a gas fitter turned midfielder from Dewsbury, who was sold to West Ham United for £60,000. My father completed both of those deals with his counterparts in the team's hotel in Southport after a Friday night game that we had lost 1-0. After that, the Football Club was in a position to pay most of its debt and A Dennis Limited got its money back. It was a measure of my father's commitment to the Football Club that he would lend it £40,000 with seemingly little or no chance that it would be repaid. Unfortunately, my father suffered a backlash at that time because Gorry and Otulakowski were two of a number of bright, young prospects at the club, and my father had gone on public record as saying that these players would be sold 'over my dead body'. Inevitably, when each one of them did depart, he was made very publicly to eat his words. My

14

father's predicament taught me a valuable lesson for the future, which was to never publicly make a commitment that you're not sure you can deliver on.

In 1973 Johnny Steele moved from the manager's office to the secretary's and Jim Iley took over as manager. Steady but unspectacular progress was achieved under Iley, whose job was made harder by the procession of talented young players being sold by the board. In addition to Gorry and Otulakowski, Mick Butler, a phenomenal goal scorer who was plucked from local league football, Bobby Doyle, a class Scottish midfielder who went on to have a great career with Peterborough, Blackpool and Portsmouth, and another local product, Mick Pickering, were all sold. But nonetheless, Iley's Barnsley, towards the end of 1976-77, were serious contenders for promotion. Unfortunately those hopes were snuffed out following a 3-4 home defeat to promotion rivals Exeter City, who came from 3-0 down to take the points. The following season another campaign that promised much finished in disappointment as the team came up short, ending the season in seventh place. For some time before the departure of Iley there had been mounting unrest amongst the fans, and chants of 'Dennis out, Iley out' would regularly ring around Oakwell. The constant pressure really got to my father, but he never considered walking away from the club. One day he and I had a chat during which he bemoaned the situation, but my response was: "If you put yourself up there to be shot at, then sometimes it's going to happen." My own words came back to haunt me many times over the years. But it remains true to this day – if you're the chairman of a football club, then you are not going to please all of the people all of the time.

After the maelstrom of financial crises that had afflicted the club during the 60s and early 70s, the work done during the Iley regime helped stablise the Football Club finances. But the driver of the club's ability to show much more ambition was the launch of the Reds' Golden Lottery Fund. Commercial Manager Brian Handley established the lottery, which very quickly turned into a money spinner for the club and at its peak was capable of generating up to £5,000 per week profit, which in those days was a very significant figure. The club had a network of agents operating throughout Barnsley and the surrounding districts selling tickets, and this was a simple yet effective way of generating finance.

Following the resignation of Jim Iley towards the end of the 1977-78 season, allowing him to take the role as manager at Blackburn Rovers, the club made its most daring and historic appointment. My father and the directors invited Leeds legend and goal scoring machine Allan Clarke to become player-manager in the summer of 1978. 'Sniffer', as he was affectionately known, was a full England international and had scored goals at the highest level throughout his career, so to get him to Oakwell was a massive coup. Swansea had appointed John Toshack from Liverpool and Barnsley were trying to do something similar by bringing in a big name. It wasn't widely known that Allan was actually second choice, as an effort to bring in the great Scottish midfielder Billy Bremner had failed. It was actually Billy who recommended Allan to the Oakwell board and Allan signed for a then club record fee of about £40,000. Bringing one of the country's best strikers into a decent, well-organised Fourth Division team was a smart yet ambitious move and with other signings such as Tommy Graham and Derek Bell, the team was transformed from also-rans to promotion favourites. Allan himself scored twelve goals that season and promotion was clinched with a victory against Grimsby Town, eventual runners-up in the league, on an emotional Tuesday night at Oakwell in front of 21,000 fans. My wife Christianne and I were living in Pogmoor and after midweek home games we used to meet friends in the Tommy Treddlehoyle on Pogmoor Road or the Grey Horse at Old Town. The night of the Grimsby game we went to both pubs and then back to our house at closing time for some further celebrations. As a wedding present we had been given some vintage champagne, which we had put down for the christening of our hoped-for first born. However, I'm ashamed to say that we drank the whole lot that night so more champagne had to be bought to celebrate the birth of our first daughter, Sarah, in 1980. Our second daughter, Caroline, came into this world in 1982, and just to set the record straight, Christianne and I had been married on 19 February 1977, at

St Paul's Church, Old Town. The old man couldn't believe that we had decided to get married in the football season, but thankfully, we only missed a 2-1 defeat at Darlington with Graham Pugh being sent off.

The joys of promotion were soon to be overshadowed by personal tragedy. It was quite widely known by this point that my father wasn't a well man. In fact, there's no easy way to say this but he had a drink problem, which had caused him to become very poorly. The many years of early mornings and long days in the fruit trade had taken its toll and it is my belief that the added pressure of the Football Club contributed to this problem. Being chairman of a football club does not feel like hard work when things are going well, but when things are not going so well there is a great deal of pressure. Typically, you don't always know when someone has a drink problem until it's too late. As a family we never really noticed the difference between my father having a glass or two of whiskey at a Christmas party to him having a couple in the evenings. The first time I took serious note of the issue was during the strawberry season one year. My father had always had very strong views about daytime drinking. He couldn't abide it, so if ever I had a few drinks on a Saturday lunchtime I knew it was in my interest not to get found out. However, one day during a particularly busy period of the summer my father came home for lunch looking absolutely shattered. My mother asked him if he'd like a gin and tonic to freshen him up and to my surprise he said yes. I did think to myself: "My father drinking in the daytime? This can't be right." But I think that was a significant moment in his life because it changed from being a one-off to help relieve the pressure of a stressful day into a daily habit that would eventually claim his life. Throughout 1979 my father had been in and out of hospital and he eventually passed away in the early hours of Monday 1 July 1979, in Barnsley and District General Hospital. His last major act as chairman was to authorise the signing, by Allan Clarke, of a certain Ronnie Glavin. Allan was very fond of my father and was a regular visitor during his illness, and it was on one of these visits to the hospital that Allan confirmed that the Glavin deal had been done.

The funeral was due to be held on the following Friday lunchtime and having operated the business as normal during the week, it was closed as a mark of respect to my father at 10am that morning. The funeral was a very moving affair with a guard of honour being provided by the players of Barnsley Football Club. Manager Allan Clarke and his coaching staff were present, as were my father's colleagues from the board as well as other dignitaries from the football world. Additionally, there were many representatives from the fruit trade in attendance as well as many of our local customers and the staff from the family business. Following the church service at St Mary's in Barnsley town centre, mourners were welcomed back to my parents' house at 15 Granville Street, where a very respectful gathering mutated into something of a drinking session, which went on until midnight. The whole afternoon acted as amazing therapy for me because there were so many people at the house that day who had known my father for many years and who spoke so warmly and respectfully about him. Listening to so many great memories and stories definitely helped to ease the pain, although I suspect the alcohol had a hand in that too. Some time before my father died he had confided in me that there had been discussions amongst directors about the prospect of bringing younger people onto the board. My father had obviously put my name forward and Ralph Potter's son, Ian, was also in the frame. After getting over the shock of my father's death I began to wonder whether the new Chairman, Geoff Buckle, and his colleagues, were still of the same mind. Then out of the blue one afternoon Geoff popped into my office to reassure me that the board was still thinking along the same lines and that he'd be in touch.

CHAPTER 3

Life on (the) Board

Throughout all of my years of following Barnsley, the team of the early 1980s was undoubtedly one of the most attractive and exciting I've ever seen. Allan Clarke had brought in good players such as Ronnie Glavin, Derrick Parker, Trevor Aylott, Ian Evans and the goalkeeper Gary Pearce. Leeds legend Norman Hunter also came to the club on a free transfer from Bristol City, and a young Ian Banks was establishing himself as a first team regular. However, Allan famously left the club after a midweek away game at Brentford to become the manager of his beloved Leeds United, taking his backroom staff of coach Barry Murphy and chief scout Martin Wilkinson – the man responsible for recommending to Allan so many good players – to Elland Road with him. The Barnsley board swiftly moved to appoint Norman Hunter as player-manager, and he was allowed to bring in more players. Stewart Barrowclough came back to the club, having been sold to Newcastle United in my father's era, and Ray McHale proved to be a very shrewd signing from Brighton & Hove Albion. This was one of the best Barnsley sides of all time, and their skill, hard work and talent was rewarded when Norman led them to promotion to the old Second Division at the end of season 1980-81 – a huge achievement and one that was seen by many supporters as the Holy Grail for Barnsley Football Club. As a group of mates and I travelled the country following our team, those far off days seem so carefree in comparison to what was to come.

The following season Norman Hunter's team continued with their expansive brand of football and I'm sure that many fans will recall an evening game at Hillsborough where for forty-five minutes Barnsley played what, in my opinion, was the best spell of football I have ever seen from a Barnsley side. We went 2-0 up and only an injury to striker Derrick Parker, disrupting the flow of the team, saved Wednesday from humiliation. The match ended 2-2 and Derrick was never quite the same player after that night. Having threatened to mount a serious challenge for promotion, the team's form deserted them towards the end of the season but still finished a very credible sixth place. Promotion hopes were undermined by a 3-2 defeat at Blundell Park on Good Friday after we had taken a two goal lead, and our hopes were finally dashed with a 2-0 reverse to Leicester City at Oakwell on a Tuesday night. The highlight of that season, though, was an amazing run in the League Cup, then known as the Milk Cup. A 9-2 aggregate win over Peterborough United set us on our way. First Division Swansea succumbed 4-3 on aggregate in the next round before another First Division outfit, Brighton & Hove Albion, were the visitors for a third round clash. Glavin, McCarthy and Aylott (two) scored the goals as we romped to a 4-1 triumph, setting up a mouth-watering fourth round clash against Manchester City at Oakwell. Myself and nearly 34,000 other people in the ground that night will still be able to picture Trevor Aylett rising majestically at the far post to power home the winner in a hard fought 1-0 victory. The fifth round saw us drawn away at Anfield to face the mighty Liverpool, the club that was dominating English football in that era. 15,000 Barnsley fans made the journey that night, battling through a thick fog to support their team. Many of those supporters did not gain admission to Anfield until half-time due to delays on the M62, but a fighting performance by battling Barnsley in the murk of Merseyside saw us earn a 0-0 draw and a replay at Oakwell the following Wednesday. The fairytale ended that night as a glittering Liverpool team ran out easy winners, 3-1, with former bin man Colin Walker notching the consolation goal for Barnsley. Colin was in the thick of it that night, not only scoring the goal but also inadvertently catching Liverpool and England defender Phil Thompson rather late resulting in a serious gash to Thompson's calf. Some years later Thompson came to Oakwell as reserve team manager of Sheffield United and was invited into the boardroom for a cup of tea to warm him up on what had been a very cold night. As my colleagues and I chatted to Phil, he reminisced about his previous visit to Oakwell and expressed the view that if he ever met that bin man again he'd sort him out. We didn't have the heart to tell him that Colin was our youth team coach at that time, and I silently prayed that Phil wouldn't bump into Colin in the corridor as he made his way to the visiting team's coach.

After such a momentous season it was extremely sad to see one or two key players leave the club. Ray McHale departed to Sheffield United, disappointed that the club had only offered him a one year extension to his contract, and Londoner Trevor Aylott moved back to his home city when he joined Millwall – a move that Trevor has since admitted that he has always regretted. That was the start of the break-up of what had been a very good team. After the success of the previous couple of seasons the 1982-83 campaign felt disappointing as the magic of the previous years gradually faded. Nonetheless, a tenth place finish was perfectly acceptable. By the following year there was a further deterioration as other members of that great team were allowed to leave. Local hero and true Oakwell legend Mick McCarthy was sold to Manchester City for £200,000 and a run of poor results saw the pressure increase on manager Hunter.

In the January of 1984 the fateful evening came when I was approached, as promised, by the club chairman, Geoff Buckle, about joining the board as a director. I was told that the board was considering myself and Barry Taylor, a man whom I'd met some years previously as we'd both served on the squash club committee at Shaw Lane, and who was a successful local businessman who ran the thriving retail outlet at Barnsley Hospital. Geoff invited us both to attend the next meeting. At the end of that conversation I broke the news to Christianne that the call that she'd been dreading since Geoff's first contact with me following my father's death had just taken place. She knew that life was going to change forever for our family, but she was also aware that it was an ambition of mine to serve on the board of the football club I loved, and she was wholehearted in her support for my decision to accept the chairman's invitation. Thankfully, the girls were then aged three and one, so they didn't have a say in it.

Barry and I then attended the board meeting the following week to be interviewed by the directors. This was a slightly surreal experience for me because all of the directors had been colleagues and friends of my father so I knew all of them well. As the meeting drew to a close the appointment of Barry and myself was ratified and I have to admit to feeling great pride knowing that I could now serve and influence my beloved Barnsley Football Club. I must also confess that having had time to think about the possibility of being a director following Geoff's contact a few years earlier, I had come to the conclusion that with the pressures of business and a young family this wasn't something I was in a rush to do. However, some opportunities in life only ever come along once so I knew I had to seize the moment. My wife was supportive, but we both knew that family life was going to change forever and that at thirty-four years of age I was going to become a very busy man.

Although I had had some insight into the workings of the Football Club, I felt that I needed to gain much more background knowledge. With that in mind I arranged a series of meetings with a man who needs little introduction to most Barnsley fans – Club Secretary Michael Spinks. Michael was, at that time, and continued to be throughout my working relationship with him, at the very centre of everything that happened at Oakwell. He was the eyes and ears of the club and knew everything and everyone. He understood the reasons behind every decision, he lived and breathed the football club, he knew all of the FA regulations back to front and all in all was a very capable man and a top football administrator. My father appointed Michael as secretary in 1977 when Johnny Steele moved from being secretary to general manager. Some years earlier I had met Michael at away matches when the sparse number of Barnsley supporters that travelled all knew each other on first name terms because there were so few of us. Following my appointment to the board, I regularly met with Michael, read board meeting minutes, asked questions based on those minutes and got as much background knowledge as I possibly could into how, why and where the club was at that particular time. In those days there was a much less formal approach to board meetings, which were only held when the chairman felt necessary. Information that was provided at the meetings was limited but to be fair that's how a lot of businesses ran in those days. The board at that time was chaired by Geoff Buckle, his vice-chairman was Arthur Raynor, and Johnny Steele, Gordon Pallister, Ralph Potter, Norman Moody and Charlie Williams were the other board members. All of these men had great Barnsley credentials and the work that was started when my father was chairman and continued by Geoff Buckle and his board provided the stability and platform for future boards of directors to build on.

On the field the team continued to struggle and within a few weeks of Barry and myself joining the board, Norman Hunter lost his job. Youth team coach Bobby Collins was appointed as caretaker manager and his appointment was ratified as permanent boss at the end of the season. It seemed to Barry and myself for a long time that this was likely to happen and we were slightly disappointed that the net wasn't cast wider, especially seeing that we had interviewed Higham-born Keith Burkinshaw, who had recently left his post as manager at Tottenham Hotspur having take them to UEFA Cup glory a few weeks earlier. However, Bobby had been a top player with Everton and Scotland in his day and was also an integral part of the Revie revolution at Leeds United. He had been a fearsomely tough-tackling midfielder who had a reputation for not taking any prisoners on the football field. His career with Leeds was prematurely ended in a Fairs Cup match against Torino when a bad tackle caused his thighbone to be broken, but Bobby went on to play and manage Hull City before being brought to Oakwell as youth team coach by Norman Hunter. My first experience of Bobby came just after I had joined the board when I went down to watch his junior team, playing in the Intermediate League one cold, damp Saturday morning on the Queen's Ground, now part of the academy. In those days families and general spectators would watch from the near side of the pitch and the coaching staff of both teams would be at the far side. Having wandered over to the far side to speak to Bobby I realised just how ferocious he could be. He put the fear of God into those lads that day, and although in the intervening years I have heard coaches dish out some fearful rollockings to players, nothing compares to what I witnessed that day. It was actually quite shocking and I hoped that this was not the norm in professional football.

The first major crisis that I came across as a director occurred during the summer of 1984 when Bobby Collins wanted to sign Gordon Owen from Cardiff City. Gordon was a Monk Bretton lad who had signed for Sheffield Wednesday as a youngster before moving to Wales. Bobby had agreed a fee with Cardiff of £30,000, but unfortunately the club had a cash flow problem. This was brought about because we had an overdraft facility of £60,000, which rose to £100,000 in the summer, but the increase each summer needed to be agreed between the chairman and the bank manager. That summer, this hadn't happened, so when Club Secretary Michael Spinks spoke to the bank to authorise the money transfer, he was politely informed that we didn't have the correct facility in place. It was further explained that not only would the bank require guarantees for the extra facility, but they were also demanding guarantees for the original sum. The club had an embarrassing situation on its hands because we had agreed to sign a player who we couldn't pay for. An emergency board meeting took place and each director agreed to sign a personal guarantee to satisfy the bank's requirements. The implication behind this, of course, meant that each director was personally liable for the sum of money that he had guaranteed in the event of the club failing financially. Sadly, at a meeting arranged with the bank, some of the long serving directors had had a change of heart and for personal reasons decided that they were unable to sign such guarantees. Myself, Mr Potter, Mr Taylor and the chairman did proceed and to the eternal credit of Barry and Geoff they agreed to make up the difference between what was available and what was required. Those directors who had decided against signing the guarantees resigned from the board, but in recognition of their service to the club and their years of hard work they were offered the position of honorary vice-presidents with directors' box privileges for as long as they wanted them. Soon afterwards Mick Hayselden, who ran a large Audi and VW car dealership, was appointed to the board and duly made the same financial commitment as the rest of us.

On the pitch the start of that season under Bobby Collins saw the team lose its first three matches. However, a 2-0 win at Notts County sparked an unlikely fifteen-match unbeaten run, which was only brought to an end by a 2-1 reverse at Oldham Athletic two days before Christmas. These results were not achieved with the free flowing football that we had seen under Norman Hunter in his early days but was functional, gritty football based on hard work and an organised defence. Centre halves Paul Futcher and Larry May had formed a formidable pairing, whilst Clive Baker in goal was inspirational. Other than a 5-1 thrashing of Wolves at Oakwell, goals were in short supply. The highlight of the season was a little cup run we had to the sixth round which started with a 4-3 home victory over Reading before Brighton & Hove Albion were dispatched 2-1 at Oakwell. For the fifth round, we were drawn away at Lawrie McMenemy's Southampton, then one of the top teams in the country. The original fixture had been postponed due to the weather so the match was played on Monday evening, 4 March after we had lost 5-3 away at Charlton two days earlier. The prize for the winners of the cup tie was a televised home game against Liverpool the following Sunday, and it was widely assumed that Southampton, featuring the likes of Peter Shilton and Joe Jordan, would emerge victorious. But Bobby Collins' brave Barnsley had other ideas and a penalty from Gordon Owen, accompanied by a goal from young striker Steve Agnew – later to be converted into an excellent midfield player – saw us home to a famous 2-1 victory. For the long journey home the Southampton directors very graciously put a case of champagne on the bus so after a great victory and a couple of glasses of champers, a long trip north flashed by. Unfortunately we couldn't repeat the heroics against Liverpool and were soundly beaten 4-0. In the league, although we had done enough to ensure mid-table safety, a three point haul from the last seven games saw the season end in alarming fashion. Even more alarming was the level to which home crowds had dropped, with the nadir being reached on 6 May when only 3,053 people witnessed a drab 0-0 draw against Wimbledon. The season ended with a 4-0 hammering at Robert Maxwell's Oxford United where the home team were crowned as champions of the division. But events at Oxford and everywhere else in English football that day were overshadowed by the horrors that had taken place at Bradford City. It was, of course, the day that tragedy struck in the shape of the Valley Parade fire when fifty-six people lost their lives with many more being injured.

That summer the decision was made to sack Bobby Collins and after much soul-searching we agreed to bring back former boss Allan Clarke. The impact that Allan had during his first stint at Oakwell had been amazing, and we hoped he could recreate that atmosphere and give Barnsley the lift we needed. It is my belief that Allan's experiences at Leeds, where he struggled as manager, had left him a little scarred. I also believe that Allan's self-confidence, which often bordered on arrogance – and I don't say that disrespectfully because it's a quality that players and managers sometimes need – had taken a severe dent. It seemed that we had a different man back and the hoped-for boost never really happened. I personally found Allan Clarke very difficult to strike a relationship with and although he had been close to my father, none of that seemed to rub off with me. To be fair to Allan there were some highlights, including a run to the fifth round of the FA Cup in season 1986-87, which resulted in a 2-0 defeat at Arsenal and an amazing 5-2 triumph away at West Ham in the League Cup in October 1987, which was memorable not just for the result and performance but for the rather gaudy yellow shirts and black shorts that Barnsley wore that night.

It was decided by the board that I would take over from Ralph Potter as the director responsible for ground safety and improvements. Following the Safety of Sports Ground Act in 1975, the legal requirements on a club such as Barnsley became even more onerous and it was important that the club adhered carefully to the directions that came from the Standing Committee for Ground Safety. The committee was made up of representatives of the local authority, South Yorkshire Police and South Yorkshire Fire and Ambulance Service. It was on the recommendations of the officers of this committee that the local authority would issue the club with its Safety Certificate, without which a club could not operate on a matchday. Michael Spinks and I were the club's representatives on this committee and it gave me great insight into the issues of safety, stadium management and crowd control. In the late 70s and early 80s, the club had spent substantial sums of money on upgrading the terraces and crush barriers at Oakwell, although to the naked eye it seemed that very little improvement had been made to the ground for years. Part of my remit from the board was to investigate the possibility of improving facilities at Oakwell. I have not-so-fond memories of wandering around the parts of Oakwell that people rarely visited, with Michael Spinks and the club's architect, Peter Landon. It always seemed to be cold and raining when we had these meetings, but we did manage to come up with a couple of schemes. The first of these was the construction of two modern toilet blocks – one for the area behind the Spion Kop and one behind the Brewery Stand. The total cost of that particular project was about £60,000, half of which was funded by a grant from the Football Grounds Improvement Trust. We also completed a project to improve the walkways behind the old Brewery Stand and the Pontefract Road End. Our next project was replacing the original Oakwell floodlights, which had first been erected in 1963. As an aside, that innovation was marked by a friendly match between Barnsley and Bolton Wanderers, with the great Tom Finney and Jimmy Hagan making guest appearances for the Reds. The estimated cost of this project was in the region of £200,000 – money we did not have. But fortunately Allan Clarke had signed a young left-back on a free transfer called John Beresford. Although John was a Sheffielder it didn't stop him being a good footballer and towards the end of season 1988-89 Beresford went to Portsmouth for £275,000. With the grant that was also available it meant that we could erect new floodlights and still have some money let over for team strengthening. I thoroughly enjoyed the role that the board had given me as it gave me real insight into the difficulties of developing Oakwell and the legal responsibilities upon the club. On one occasion, in 1989, I became very much aware of those responsibilities prior to a fourth round cup tie against Everton. The club's Safety Certificate specified the maximum permitted levels of attendance in each area of the ground and a major concern for Michael Spinks and myself was that the old Spion Kop could legally house over 9,000 people. It had been decided that for the Everton game the Kop was to be reserved for travelling fans, and there was a serious demand for tickets from Merseyside. After Michael and I made representations to the board, it was decided that in spite of the legally agreed limit, it would have been unsafe to release that number of tickets and the figure was set at 7,500. Although I was disappointed that day that the team had lost 1-0, it was the first time in my life as a director that I had been more concerned about crowd safety than the result, and was very relieved that the afternoon passed without incident despite a crowd in excess of 32,000.

On the field Allan's second coming hadn't really had the desired affect and although we achieved a mid-table finish in season 1985-86, a horrendous start to the following season, which saw us lose the first six games on the spin, left us going into our New Year's Day away fixture at Hull City anchored to the bottom of the table with a mere sixteen points. Myself and fellow Directors Chris Harrison and Mick Hayselden met at my office near the football ground prior to a pre-Christmas board meeting to demand the dismissal of the manager. But our older colleagues, Barry Taylor, Ralph Potter and Chairman Buckle, headed off this coup. They were proved to be right as a remarkable second half of that season saw us climb to eleventh position in the league. Allan showed a marked reluctance to spend money that the board would make available. This attitude could occasionally be somewhat frustrating and perversely was demonstrated by what turned out to be one of his better signings. Barnsley fans will fondly remember David Currie, who we signed during the 1987-88 season. At the time there were three players in the old Fourth Division who were making a big name for themselves – David Platt, at Crewe, Chester's Stuart Rimmer, and David Currie of Darlington. For a change we actually had a few bob in the bank and in the view of the directors we needed to sign a goal scorer. The chairman had suggested to Allan that he ought to bring in a striker, but got nowhere. Barry Taylor and I asked the chairman for his permission to go and discuss the matter with Allan ourselves, and during that conversation asked him which of the three – Platt, Rimmer and Currie – he would prefer. He plumped for Currie, but said he wouldn't be prepared to spend more than £40,000, which was much less than Darlington's asking price of £100,000. As it happened we actually had pretty good connections at Darlington. First team coach Eric Winstanley was good mates with their manager Dave Booth, once a team mate of Eric's at Barnsley, and I knew one of Darlington's directors, Alan Moore, with whom I did business occasionally and whose father had been a contemporary chairman of my father's. Between us we managed to talk Darlington down to £90,000, but in spite of the fact that Barry and I had told Allan that we would have it minuted that the board were prepared to authorise and take responsibility for this signing, he still insisted that the price was too high. Nothing happened but towards the end of February, following a 1-0 defeat away at Sheffield United, where our striking resources had been further depleted by the sending off of Roger Wilde, a small protest at the lack of activity in the transfer market greeted the team bus on its arrival back at Oakwell from Bramall Lane. The manager responded by seeking permission to try to sign David Currie. Early the following week I was very surprised to pick up the *Yorkshire Post* and read the headline: "Clarke gets his man," with the article explaining that Allan had been tracking David all season and he'd got a real bargain at a mere £150,000 – some bargain. To be fair to Allan, despite the fact that we paid more than we needed to, David was a great signing for Barnsley Football Club, scoring some valuable goals and bringing a little bit of magic to Oakwell in what had otherwise been a very mundane season. Over the summer of 1988 Allan Clarke brought in striker Steve Cooper to join David Currie. Steve had been an international high jumper in his school days and his aerial ability alongside Currie gave us a real threat up front. Older fans will remember Cooper's goal celebration after he'd scored the winner in a fourth round cup replay against Stoke City at Oakwell in January 1989 when he produced the most amazing backflip, which featured for many months as part of the intro to *Match of the Day*. In Mel Machin's time we had an enquiry from Bobby Gould, then the manager of Wimbledon, who indicated he might pay £500,000 for Cooper. Bobby said he'd get back to us to firm things up, but we never heard from him again. Some years later, when Bobby was a guest in the Oakwell boardroom, Vice-Chairman Barry Taylor reminded him of the story and asked why he hadn't pursued his initial interest. Bobby replied that he was quite keen to sign the player but his policy before any transfer was to watch the player concerned from the terraces so that he could gauge the opinion from the home fans about any prospective recruit. Apparently, Bobby had attended a game at Oakwell one day, paying his money and standing in the old Brewery Stand, but decided that he wouldn't go ahead with the transfer because of the relatively low opinion that Barnsley fans around him had of Steve Cooper. I doubt whether many managers were quite as quirky as Bobby Gould in going about their business this way, but there is a certain logic to it that has to be admired. Currie's sixteen goals helped the club to finish in seventh position in Division Two that season, with three wins from the last three games seeing us fall just short of the play-off places. However, whatever optimism there may have been at Oakwell and throughout football had been extinguished by the appalling events that had taken place down the road from us at Hillsborough on 15 April that year. Cleverer and wiser men than I have passed judgements on the terrible events of that tragic day, but suffice it to say it was clear that football would never be the same again.

CHAPTER 4

Mr Chairman

The 1989-90 campaign didn't start well for Barnsley with the team struggling near to the foot of the table. Matters came to a head on Saturday 4 November after we had lost 1-0 at home to Portsmouth. The crowd was low and the performance was poor. After the game, when the visiting directors had departed, I suggested to Geoff Buckle that we needed to meet to discuss the situation. Geoff was not enthusiastic about this. However, he said that if that was the will of the rest of the directors then he would accept that, but left it up to me to make the arrangements. On the Sunday morning I had a ring around and it was agreed that we would meet at my house in Granville Street on the Monday evening at 6pm. Late on the Monday afternoon I rang Michael Spinks to tell him that an unofficial board meeting had been arranged for that evening and Michael took the opportunity to inform me that Sheffield Wednesday had been in touch with Allan Clarke about David Currie. David was our star turn at that time and although there had been much transfer speculation surrounding him, this was the first time that there had been a firm inquiry that the board was aware of. Apparently, Allan had agreed with Wednesday's manager, Ron Atkinson, that we would be happy with a deal whereby we would receive £100,000 cash plus Wednesday players Steve Whitton and Imre Varadi. I was of the opinion that if we were going to sell Currie, we should be doing a cash deal so that the manager could bring in players that he actually wanted.

At the board meeting that evening, none of the directors were aware that Allan had been talking to Sheffield Wednesday about Currie, so I started proceedings by giving them the news. After much discussion it became clear that rather than a general conversation about the next steps we were in reality talking about Allan's future. Geoff crystalised everybody's thoughts by saying that we either had to back him or sack him. He then followed that up by adding that if we sacked him, then he would resign. Geoff was in a difficult position because he and his wife, Barbara, had become quite friendly with Alan and his wife, Margaret. But it was certainly a shock when he dropped the bombshell. The whole of the meeting had been tense, and tensions stretched even further when Chris Harrison responded to Geoff by saying: "Well if you do go, we'll ask John Dennis to be chairman." That was another unexpected bombshell because, contrary to received opinion since then, there had been no discussion along those lines beforehand and there had been no plotting in smoke-filled rooms. As the meeting progressed it became clear which way things were going and that Allan's job hung by a thread. Individually, each director came to the conclusion that we needed a change of manager, but that we did not need an inexperienced chairman to guide the club through what was going to be a turbulent period. We pleaded with Geoff to reconsider his position, but he remained adamant. After further discussion Geoff left the meeting, leaving the rest of us to consider the implications behind what had been said. It was agreed that further representations should be made to Geoff, but that should his stance remain unchanged then I would become the chairman of Barnsley Football Club subject to me discussing the matter with my wife and family. My overriding concern was that I found myself in the same position as when I first became a director, where a once in a lifetime opportunity was presenting itself to me, but at a far earlier stage of my life than I had expected or anticipated. After all, I was only thirty-nine years of age, and that would have made me one of the youngest, if not the youngest, chairman of the ninety-two Football League clubs. As a further complication I had to be off to London on business early the following morning, but hoped that the speculation linking Allan Clarke with the vacant Hull City job would turn into reality. That would have been an easy way out of our difficulties. But that was not to be, as it was announced on the radio as I drove back up the M1 that Hull had appointed Stan Ternent as their new manager. Within minutes of arriving home I received a call from Barry Taylor, who confirmed that, after reflection, the rest of the board were prepared to stand by the decisions that had been reached the previous evening. He made it clear that the other directors were in full support of my prospective appointment as chairman, so it was left that I would speak to Geoff one more time to try and get him to change his mind, but that in any event we needed an official board meeting as early as possible the following day to ratify the termination of Allan's contract and possibly to confirm my appointment as chairman. That meeting took place in the boardroom on the Wednesday morning, 8 November, and with very little further discussion required, both decisions were confirmed. However, the outgoing chairman felt that it was his duty to confirm the decision to Allan, although Allan was perfectly well aware of what was happening. As the new chairman I felt slightly uncomfortable with this arrangement, so it was agreed that I would accompany Geoff to Allan's office to deliver the bad news.

I have to admit that presiding over Allan Clarke's sacking was a strange moment. My father had appointed him in 1978 and he had done so much good for the Football Club, particularly in that first spell. He had been an icon of British football, and here was I watching him being sacked. In all fairness to Allan his second stint at Barnsley had been punctuated by the regular sales of his better players. Larry May went to Sheffield Wednesday for £200,000, Stuart Gray joined Aston Villa for £175,000 and, of course, a young David Hirst went to our neighbours at Hillsborough for a basic fee of £200,000. The club had also negotiated two further add-ons for Hirst, one of £25,000 if David made ten appearances for England Under 21s, with a further £25,000 being due should he become a full England international. He made the necessary Under 21 appearances so Barnsley got the extra £25,000, and I remember the day well when he made his England debut. I had just got in from work one Saturday afternoon and switched the television on to see some grainy pictures of England vs Australia on a summer tour in 1991. I immediately rang Michael Spinks at home to tell him to get an invoice off to Sheffield Wednesday first thing Monday morning, to be told by his mother that Michael had gone back to the office. By then I knew that Michael had already beaten me to the punch and this was confirmed when I duly spoke to him and he patiently asked me what I thought he was doing back at work on a Saturday afternoon and that the invoice had already been typed and would be in the post that evening.

The dismissal of Allan Clarke was made even more surreal because I was also witnessing the departure of Geoff Buckle, the man who had supported my father twenty-three years previously when they stepped in to help save Barnsley Football Club. They had become good friends as well as working colleagues and I had a huge amount of respect for Geoff. He had presided over some great times at Oakwell and it was distressing that he had taken the decision to step down from the board. He was, of course, offered directors' box privileges as befitting a man who had given so much of his life to Barnsley Football Club, but sadly he was only to avail himself of those privileges on a couple of occasions in the years to come. Allan and Geoff had a glass of champagne and offered me one, but that was the last thing on my mind as I knew that I needed to have a clear head to deal with my new-found position of authority. As I returned to the boardroom I started to realise for the first time the weight of responsibility that I had taken on my shoulders, but knew that my remaining colleagues – Barry Taylor, Ralph Potter, Mick Hayselden and Chris Harrison – would support me in any way possible. The first task was to appoint a caretaker manager, with the obvious choice being Eric Winstanley. Eric had been a terrific servant to the Football Club over the years and was Allan's first team coach. I left the board meeting again to seek out Eric and, unsurprisingly, he was delighted to assist in any way that he could. He made it clear to me that he felt we needed to bring one or two players in to freshen things up and was concerned about his future employment prospects at the club when a new manager was appointed. It was agreed that he would be permitted to bring in loan signings and that we as a board would do our utmost to ensure that Eric's employment was safe. After further discussions with my directors we agreed to advertise the post of manager for Barnsley Football Club, and the search was on.

After the meeting broke up I rang my wife to confirm the good news. I also rang the business to tell them that I wouldn't be back that day and a whole new phase of my life had started. I felt very proud but very apprehensive and as the phone started to ring with enquiries for the now vacant manager's position – the grapevine worked even in those days – it was a very strange feeling being referred to as chairman. On that long drive back from London the previous day I had made my mind up about how I would try and tackle the job. I was determined not to be Ernest Dennis MK2 – and I mean no disrespect to my father when I say that and obviously I was not daft enough to ignore the way that he had gone about the job – but I wanted to be my own man. I felt it was important to bring dignity to the job without being too starchy. I wanted to make myself approachable, both inside the Football Club and out. I wanted to re-affirm our roots in the community because without the support of the local people we could not succeed, and I wanted to strengthen our relationship with the local authority, which had become quite strained over the years. I felt it was important that the club should be well represented in the world of football and to voice strong opinions on all footballing issues. And of course, more than anything, I wanted the club to be successful.

The board had made it clear that following Allan's departure we would not be rushed into an appointment, but nonetheless through various football contacts such as journalists and friends of friends, different names of potential managers came to the fore. One of those was John Rudge, who was doing a fantastic job at Port Vale. Although over the next couple of weeks we received a high number of applications – both written and verbal – it didn't mean very much because not all of those applications could be taken seriously. I am always slightly cynical when I hear chairmen or chief executives boasting to their fans about how many hundreds of people have applied for their vacant manager's job, because my experience taught me that whilst that number of letters might have been received, genuinely appointable applications were few and far between. In fact, you could normally divide your applications into three piles. The first would be a small number of genuine possibilities; the second – much larger – would be made up of those who had been involved in the game but who, for a variety of reasons, did not meet our criteria; the third pile always used to make me chuckle, as it would contain totally ridiculous applications, ranging from Boy Scout football team managers to out and out pranksters who were trying to take the mickey.

When the board met a few days later to discuss the vacant manager's position, we sifted through the formal applications and, although there were some impressive names, such as ex-players Ronnie Glavin, Barry Murphy, David Booth, experienced out of work managers Mick Buxton, Alan Dicks, Colin Appleton and young manager Martin O'Neill, we kept coming back to John Rudge. I was authorised by the directors to make an official approach to Port Vale Football Club to seek permission to speak to John. I rang the Port Vale chairman, a man by the name of Bill Bell, who was a successful motor trader in the Potteries with whom I became very friendly in future years. I was somewhat taken aback by his response, which went something along the lines of: "Why would I let you do that? John and I have been negotiating a new contract for the last few weeks and he's about to sign it today. But the leaks in the media about Barnsley's so-called interest in him has cost me a few quid more than I'd have expected. So no, you can't speak to him!" With that, the phone went dead. I was very deflated because I had failed at the first hurdle, but it did teach me a valuable lesson. It was reasonable to suppose that Barnsley's managerial vacancy may have been used as a tool by John in his contract discussions with his chairman, so I realised that in future I would need to be a little bit more devious when approaching these situations.

It was back to the drawing board for the new chairman of Barnsley and his directors, but out of the blue came the sacking by Manchester City of Mel Machin. I had met Mel some years earlier when he was the first team coach at Norwich City and I'd been impressed by his general demeanour. His sacking by the Maine Road Board was a big surprise in football because only a few weeks previously he had inspired City to a 5-1 thrashing of their great rivals Manchester United. He was a very well known figure in football at that time, and I thought he'd make a great appointment for Barnsley. The board shared my view and I was once again authorised to make a move. Having sifted through all the other CVs yet again, the board considered that the only other possibility – and this was to be our fallback position should Machin turn us down – was a certain Martin O'Neill. His application was most impressive, but the feeling on the board was that a manager with more experience was needed to take the club forward. My next step was to get in touch with Mel, and if he wasn't interested we would talk to O'Neill. It was with some trepidation that I called Mel as I wasn't particularly optimistic that he'd be interested in the Barnsley job. But from the start he was a perfect gentleman and although very guarded did express some interest in the position. His caution came from the fact that he was unable to enter into serious discussions immediately because he was still in negotiations with Manchester City about his compensation, and he didn't want anything to jeopardise that. We agreed that we would keep in touch and when he'd sorted out the situation at City we would arrange to meet. But time was marching on and we were starting to come under some pressure to make an appointment. We were in the situation where we had a plan but were unable to reveal it because of Mel's need for confidentiality. Fortunately, the club was in safe hands with Eric in charge, although it didn't really feel like that at 5pm on Saturday 11 November following my first match in charge as chairman. We were away at West Bromwich Albion and we had the sort of result that nightmares are made of. There had been a new mood of optimism on the team coach that day as most of the directors and all of the first team squad, including injured players, had travelled to the Hawthorns. We stopped for the usual pre-match meal at the Post House in West Bromwich and I had a feeling it was going to be a memorable day. I wasn't wrong. We got thumped 7-0, and as I sat there watching this horror story unfold I had visions of my first game as chairman beating the club's record 9-0 defeat. The West Bromwich directors, who we got to know very well in time to come, were rightly delighted by their team's performance but managed to show some sympathy towards us. In the ensuing years every visit to the Hawthorns brought a predictable reminder from one of their directors as to what had happened on my first match as chairman. They particularly used to focus on my comment when I received the official notification of the size of the crowd when they claim that I said: "Is that the crowd or the score?"

After the debacle at West Brom, Eric was allowed to bring in two players on loan – Mark Smith, a former Sheffield Wednesday centre-half who was, at the time, at Plymouth Argyle and who Mel Machin later signed for £80,000, and a right-wing back from Derby named Brian McCord, who was a football character if ever you met one. Mel eventually signed Brian as well, but his Oakwell career never really flourished. During one of his spells when he was out of favour we had an enquiry from Bradford City, who wanted to take him on loan. The manager spoke to Brian, pointing out it'd be a great chance for him to kick-start his career. Brian's response is one I'll never forget. He said: "Well, it's a good offer from Bradford, but I'm quite settled in my life at the moment. I play for the reserves in midweek games and go off fishing and have a relaxing time on Saturdays, so I'd rather stay here if that's okay." Another infamous tale about Brian came when the *Sheffield Star*'s Trevor Lovett sent a photographer to Oakwell to take a picture of a German striker who was on trial. The photographer went to the players' lounge before one game and asked to see the German lad. But the quick thinking Brian suddenly changed his accent to a dodgy German one and told this poor unfortunate that he was the foreign trialist. The photos were duly taken, finding their way back to Trevor Lovett's desk and were eventually passed to the editor of the *Sheffield Star*, who was less than pleased that his photographer had been the victim of a practical joke. I received an angry phone call one afternoon to say that he didn't find it funny is putting it mildly. Unfortunately, I had great difficulty in responding in the appropriate chairman-like manner because I could barely hold back my laughter. Sadly, Brian's career ended in tragedy some years later when a horrific tackle from a Swansea City player resulted in him being carried off injured when he was playing for Stockport County. He actually took legal action over the challenge, and it was widely publicised that he came out of it with £250,000 compensation. Not only was Eric allowed to bring in players, but he was also instrumental in selling a player. That came about when Ray McHale, our former midfielder who was managing Scarborough FC, offered £50,000 for striker Darren Foreman. My feeling was that in our current situation, selling a promising young player like Foreman wasn't wise but that the more experienced John McDonald, who had featured rarely in the first team all season, could go. Initially, John came back from Scarborough without signing, but during a reserve game at Oakwell that evening, Ray's persuasive powers and the presence of myself and Eric Winstanley convinced John that a move to the coast was in his best interest. He duly signed on the dotted line just in time to be able to line-up for his new club against York City in the big local derby that Friday night, and we banked a welcome £50,000.

I then received the phone call that I was desperate for, from Mel Machin, to tell me that his compensation package had been agreed with Manchester City so he was in a position to speak to us. After initial contract discussions had taken place, Mel and I had a meeting at my home in Cawthorne on Boxing Day. We immediately hit it off and we finalised the contract negotiations subject to them being ratified by the rest of the board. I had arranged a ticket for Mel to go to the game against Watford that afternoon. I had hoped he wouldn't be recognised by the fans, although to be fair, his traditional flat cap made him blend quite well with the Barnsley faithful! The board formally ratified the contract that Mel and I had discussed, and Mel Machin was appointed as manager of Barnsley Football Club. His first match was against Leeds United, on 30 December at Oakwell, which we won 1-0 with the goal coming from a miss-hit shot from Darren Foreman from just inside the box.

The early experience of trying to appoint a manager taught me lots of lessons along the way. I realised very quickly that the official channels of making formal approaches for managers and players of other football clubs could be sometimes seen as naïve. But of more concern to me was the fact that Barnsley Football Club needed to avoid any potential humiliation by very public rejection of our interest. Over the years my *modus operandi* changed in that I would do my homework on any potential targets, making unofficial contact to assess their interest in coming to Barnsley before then making the decision to pursue them through official channels. In football, this is quaintly known as 'tapping up', and was something that was rife when I was chairman and I'm sure will be as common in the modern era. The rules of the Football Association are very clear on this subject, but in my view, are almost unenforceable. A further lesson that I learned during my time as a young director was that the manager's contract needed to be clear and transparent. In the cases of Norman Hunter, Bobby Collins and Allan Clarke there were no specific provisions in the contract in the event of that contract being terminated. The way the termination of those contracts had been handled made me believe that we needed to have a clear understanding with any future manager as to what compensation may be payable should the contract be terminated. In future years, the board and I agreed a policy whereby a manager would receive no more than one full year's salary should he be dismissed, but that if the manager broke his contract then the club would likewise be entitled to receive one year's salary from him or his new employer. The view was taken, quite cynically I suppose, that we were more likely to be sacking a manager than him breaking his contract and going elsewhere. Additionally, given the fact that in Mel Machin's case, his salary was in the region of £40,000 per year, dismissing him early in his contract could have had serious consequences for the finances of the Football Club.

CHAPTER 5

The Machin Era

For a young and inexperienced chairman, Mel Machin was an ideal man to work with as my first manager. He was a proper football man and helped me to gain real insight into the running of a football club. However, for the relationship between the chairman and the manager – one of the most important relationships in any football club – to work, it was vital that clear lines of communication were agreed and adhered to. After a chat with the other directors, they felt comfortable that all business matters concerning the playing side of the Football Club should come through me as the board's representative. Many years earlier, I had seen my father's relationship with Jim Iley be undermined by Jim's closeness to another director, and although I wasn't a control freak, I didn't want my own position to be similarly undermined. Throughout my time as chairman I always worked hard at building a strong relationship with all of the managers with whom I worked.

After his fairytale start against Leeds, Mel then got down to assessing his squad and made it clear that he needed to strengthen it in order to help us in our battle against relegation, the minimum target that we had discussed with Mel on his appointment. We didn't have a fortune to spend, but in our pre-appointment discussions with Mel, we had assured him that we would do our best to fund new signings, and that situation was helped greatly by the sale of David Currie to Nottingham Forest. Following the departure of Allan Clarke, Ronnie Fenton, assistant to Brian Clough, and former Reds' goalkeeper Alan Hill, Cloughie's chief scout, were taking a keen interest in Currie.

In early January, I got a call from Mel to say that, subject to board approval, he had done a deal with Forest, who would give us either a straight £750,000 for David Currie, or a part cash/player swap where we would get £550,000 plus Phil Starbuck. Mel preferred the swap deal, whereas I wanted the cash. Starbuck, however, turned down the opportunity to come to Barnsley, but Mel was assured by Ronnie Fenton that the cash deal would still go through. Much to my surprise one morning, I received a phone call in my office from Brian Clough who, in a very forthright manner, informed me that Starbuck had turned down Barnsley and that the deal was off. I, in turn, protested that we had been assured by his assistant manager that the £750,000 cash deal would still go through, to which Cloughie replied: "My assistant manager doesn't have the right or the authority to say that, but if you still want a deal, we'll take Currie, but you're only getting £700,000." I asked Mr Clough to speak to Mel personally as Mel had been doing the deal on our behalf, and finally it went through at the stated £700,000. David Currie was very keen to go to Forest because he got his wages doubled to £90,000 per year plus a signing-on fee.

This gave the opportunity for Mel to make one or two signings, the first of which was young Irishman Gerry Taggart, who cost £70,000 from Manchester City. Taggart could play left-back or centre-half and was a huge, physical presence and a great footballer. He went on to become a cult hero at Oakwell, eventually being sold to Bolton Wanderers for £1million. Mel's next signing was striker Andy Saville for £80,000 from Walsall. Mel had actually gone to watch Stuart Rimmer but was hugely impressed by Saville, a big, fit strong lad with a great physique. His hold-up play was excellent and he'd got the odd goal in him too. Mel returned to his former club, Manchester City, for a second time to bring in Irish international Gary Fleming. Gary had started his career at Nottingham Forest and was a regular in the Irish squad. Initially we couldn't match the salary he was getting at Maine Road but by structuring the transfer fee in such a way that City could give him a part of it as a bonus, Gary was happy to come and play for Mel Machin. The start of his Oakwell career saw Gary feature at right-back, but he was converted by the manager into a sweeper playing behind the two centre halves – a role in which he was a revelation. Gary's career was sadly ended prematurely in 1995 following a serious knee injury, although he was to make a couple of further appearances at Oakwell as the first team physiotherapist for Nottingham Forest some years later. The fourth permanent signing that Mel made during that period was striker Brendan O'Connell, from Exeter, for £45,000. Brendan wasn't particularly prolific as a goal scorer, but Mel converted him to a midfield role, and his determination and energy went to making Brendan a great servant to Barnsley Football Club, appearing more than 250 times for the first team. Following his retirement from football, he began a career in business and I was pleased to hear recently that he has been very successful.

As the season progressed, the struggle against relegation became ever more tense but a tremendous 2-1 away win at Leeds was a major step towards avoiding the drop. The atmosphere at Elland Road that night was particularly menacing and even sitting in the directors' box was an intimidating experience. Two masterly substitutions from manager Machin – at least that's what Mel said afterwards! – made the difference as Archdeacon and O'Connell both came on to score. This was the second time I'd seen the Reds win at Elland Road since being a director, the first coming in my early days on the board when a goal apiece from Ronnie Glavin and on-loan England striker David Johnson saw us home 2-1 on a bitterly cold February afternoon. I particularly remember the occasion for another reason, which was meeting the Leeds United President, the Earl of Harwood. Myself and Barry Taylor, as new boys to football, were standing on the fringes of the assembled group in the Leeds United boardroom when the Earl of Harwood made his entrance. Although he didn't know us from Adam, he came across for a chat and, commenting on the weather conditions that day, passed the observation that there had been a touch of snow on the estate that morning. Quick as a flash, Barry, who lived on a very pleasant housing development in, to use estate agent speak, one of the more sought-after villages to the west of Barnsley, replied: "Yes, and there was some snow on our estate this morning too!" The following Saturday, a hard-earned point from a 2-2 draw at the Hawthorns with O'Connell once more finding the net sent us to Ayresome Park to face Middlesbrough on the Tuesday night for what was the proverbial 'six pointer'. Mel played five across the back, four in midfield with Andy Saville up front on his own, and a rare Mark Smith goal gave us a 1-0 win. The Barnsley contingent was in jubilant mood, a mixture of delight and relief in equal measures. I thought I'd go over to the travelling Barnsley faithful at the end of the game and applaud their support – a move that ended with me getting in trouble with the police. As I approached the Barnsley following, the ground commander accused me of trying to cause a riot and threatened to have me thrown out of the ground. I must make it clear that the Barnsley fans behaved perfectly and showed no sign of being anything other than delighted at the team's win. This wasn't the only time I locked horns with authority that season. Some weeks earlier, away at Leicester City, I behaved rather foolishly. We had been winning the game 2-0 before the referee on that day, a Mr Ray Lewis from Great Buckham, took a hand in matters, sending off first striker Steve Cooper and then Gerry Taggart. I was incensed and could feel our survival prospects diminish as we drew 2-2. The vice-chairman, sitting next to me in the directors' box, urged me to stand up for our club by having a 'chat' with the referee after the game – I really ought to have known better. At the final whistle, I hurried down to the referee's room before knocking on the door and barging in, voicing my frustration at his performance. I was careful not to use bad language, but that cut no ice with Mr Lewis, who reported me to the Football Association and I was charged with misconduct, found guilty and warned as to my future conduct. The first fans' protest that I had to endure came during that season when three supporters ran onto the pitch during a home game carrying a banner saying: "Is Dennis a menace for promotion?" Obviously they were ejected from the ground and I then discovered that one of the culprits was actually one of my own employees at A Dennis Ltd. I was absolutely fuming about this, but wiser councils advised me I could do nothing about it, so the lad kept his job.

On a personal note, in early May, my family suffered a major tragedy when my beloved mother suddenly died of a brain haemorrhage. On the Tuesday night, I had been to the Player of the Year Dinner at Ardsley House and feeling a bit rough the next morning decided to head off to Birmingham for a bit of a lazy day at a fruit trade exhibition. I called at the office on my way home to be told by my General Manager Derek Richardson that he and my family had been trying to contact me all day because my mother had been taken seriously ill. It transpired that she had suffered a massive brain haemorrhage and that Christianne had to break into her bungalow in Pogmoor so that the emergency services could attend. Sadly, she never regained consciousness and passed away on the Thursday. Mother, had she survived, would have been devastated by the news in March 1991 that the family business, A Dennis Ltd, had gone into receivership. The fruit business had always been very profitable but my elder brother had urged us to diversify into a parcels distribution project. The strategy should have been a good one but sadly, it didn't work out. Fortunately, I was able to find a group of local businesspeople who were prepared to invest with me to buy the fresh produce side of the business from the receivers, and on 27 April 1991, John Dennis Barnsley Ltd was born. I will always be grateful to that small group of men and I'm pleased to say that the new business traded successfully for many years and my investors' faith in me was repaid many times over.

The summer of 1990 saw very few additions to the squad, although striker Andy Rammell joined from Manchester United for £100,000, with a part of that transfer fee going to his first club, non-league Atherstone United, who then used their windfall to build a new stand, which was named after Rammell. During the autumn of season 1990-91, Mel came to the board with a request to sign a player called Phil Gridelet, later to be known by the Barnsley fans as 'God' – they knew he was there but they never saw him – for £175,000 from non-league Barnet. Phil had a reputation as being one of the best players outside the Football League and had played for England at semi-professional level. However, his career at Barnsley was blighted by a succession of injuries and he was allowed to leave on a free transfer three years later having made just six appearances. Although his signing had been authorised by the board, it really was the biggest mistake of Mel's time at Oakwell. Stuart Rimmer was signed on transfer deadline day from Walsall and the season ended with the team finishing in a very creditable eighth position in the league.

Notwithstanding events on the pitch, football in general was faced with many harsh realities. Following the horrors of the Bradford fire in 1985 and the Heysel disaster later that year, the further appalling tragedy at Hillsborough in 1989 left the reputation of English football in tatters. Famously, the *Sunday Times* described the game as being 'a slum sport, played in slum stadia for slum people'. In the aftermath of the Hillsborough disaster, the Lord Chief Justice of England and Wales, Peter Taylor, was commissioned to produce a report into the events of Hillsborough that spring afternoon and to make recommendations to avoid such further tragedies. The Taylor Report contained many recommendations, the most telling of which was the requirement for every football stadium operating in the top two divisions being required to become all-seater within three years. The Taylor Report was actually the first document to place greater emphasis on crowd safety and comfort rather than on merely crowd control. The report was published in early 1990 and we at Barnsley knew that we had to conform. It was suggested at the time that Barnsley was against the all-seater recommendation, but that isn't strictly true. The fact was that Oakwell only had seating capacity for 2,500 people and that no major development had taken place on the stadium since the early 1950s. We found ourselves in a position of knowing that there was a £1 million grant available from the Football Trust to assist clubs as they converted their stadiums to all-seats, but we were struggling to provide the additional funding required. A deputation from the club made up of myself, my fellow Director Ian Potter and our General Manager Michael Spinks, went to London to lobby the then Secretary of State for National Heritage, Peter Brooke, within whose department responsibility for sport fell, at his Trafalgar

Square offices to plead for more time. Without special dispensation we needed a miracle.

Somebody up above must have been listening to our prayers, because at the end of the 1991 season we received the biggest ever transfer fee in the history of the club as Carl Tiler took the same journey to Nottingham Forest that David Currie had taken the year earlier. The deadly duo of Ronnie Fenton and Alan Hill had once again been sent by Brian Clough to check out one of our players and during that season, they might as well have had season tickets for Oakwell because they attended games so regularly. Carl had developed into a commanding and cultured centre-back, even though it was a stroke of luck that he was on the books in the first place. One of our youth team players at the time, Jonathan Bond, lived in the same village as Carl Tiler and asked the youth team staff whether Carl could come down to train with us. He created a great impression immediately and was invited to sign on the dotted line. By the March of 1991, acting on the recommendations of Fenton and Hill, Brian Clough offered Mel Machin £1million for Carl Tiler. Mel rang me to tell me of Cloughie's offer and he very strongly recommended that the board turn it down, being adamant that if we held our nerve then we'd get more. This I reluctantly agreed to, but wasn't looking forward to having to explain to the board what we had done. But I kept faith with my manager, even though that faith was starting to evaporate on the basis that we never saw Fenton and Hill again that season. I was beginning to feel that the moment had passed and we'd dropped one of the biggest clangers in the club's history. But in May, Mel was to be vindicated because on the morning of the 1991 FA Cup Final between Nottingham Forest and Spurs, Mel had a call from Brian Clough offering £1.5million for Carl Tiler. Mel and his wife, Jo, had joined my wife and I at the Tower Hotel in London prior to us heading off to the Cup Final. I'd always thought it odd that Cloughie was doing big transfer deals on the morning of a Cup Final in which his team was involved, but I wasn't complaining.

Also that summer, Steve Agnew was sold to Blackburn Rovers. Mel had turned down an initial bid from the Rovers manager Don Mackay of £600,000, telling him we wouldn't take less than

£750,000. On that particular afternoon, I was attending the annual speech day at my daughters' school in Wakefield where both girls were due to receive prizes. The school secretary approached me to say there was a phone call for me in her office from a Mr Machin. To my wife's horror, I sneaked out to take the call, and Mel related the interest in Aggie from Blackburn. Mackay had previously told Mel that his Chairman, Bill Fox, would now be taking over the negotiations and asked if I could ring Bill. I knew Bill very well because not only was he the President of the Football League, but was also in the same business as myself in Lancashire. When I got back to my office later that afternoon, Bill and I had a long and lively discussion, but we finally agree a deal at £700,000 so Steve Agnew was off to Blackburn. Steve had been converted from a striker to a midfield player by Allan Clarke, after the directors had pleaded with Allan not to release him on a free transfer during the mid 1980s. He then went on to repay the club's faith in him by developing into a really talented midfield player, having seemingly recovered from the string of injuries that had dogged him as a young man. Sadly, however, on his debut for Blackburn he picked up an ankle injury and was sidelined for some time. We were shocked when that autumn we received a letter from the Ewood Park Club's solicitors threatening to sue us because they felt that we had misrepresented the player. Fortunately, Football League regulations dictate that when a buying club signs a player, it must sign a form stating its satisfaction with the fitness and health of that player, so Blackburn, thankfully, didn't have a leg to stand on (a bit like Steve Agnew!). I'm pleased to say that Steve made a full recovery from that setback and played for many years after that in an impressive career at Leicester City and Sunderland. He was always a model professional, and it's very pleasing to see a former Barnsley player doing so well in his career as a player and coach.

The implication behind these deals meant that the club was now in a position to begin the first stage of the redevelopment of Oakwell. We had already had detailed discussions with the club's architects, and their remit was simple. We needed as many seats as we could get for our money, twelve hospitality boxes and other hospitality areas. We had already opened negotiations to buy the half of the old brewery site that stretched from behind the Brewery Stand down to Pontefract Road. When those negotiations were completed for £375,000 and the architects' plans were finalised, we were then in a position to begin the construction of the 7,500-seater East Stand development. At that time, there was some debate as to whether a construction of this size was too ambitious, but the view of the board was that in the short-term, we had no idea where the money would come from for the next stage of any development, so we needed as many seats as we could get as quickly as possible. From a long-term view point, we felt that should we restrict potential attendances at Oakwell by building smaller constructions with lesser capacities, then we would probably be consigning our beloved Barnsley to the lower reaches of the Football League forever. Interestingly, we did briefly consider the possibility of relocating from Oakwell, but for emotional and financial considerations this was deemed impractical. The major stumbling block to any move away from Oakwell centred upon a condition in the sale agreement from the Senior family to the Football Club in 1908 surrounding part of the land on which the pitch and stadium stood. In simple terms, the vendor stipulated that should Oakwell cease to be used for the purposes of playing football then he and future generations of his family would have the right to buy back the land for the same price as it was sold to the Football Club for in 1908 – a figure of £1,200. This clause, known as a reversion right, was legally enforceable until twenty-five years after the death of Mr Senior's last surviving grandchild. Over the years, my board made a number of attempts to negotiate a buy-out of this clause, but the expectations of the beneficiaries were far greater than the actual commercial value.

The East Stand development began in the summer of 1992 and was completed by the following March. With the old Brewery Stand demolished there was a very strange atmosphere as we welcomed West Ham United to start the 1992-93 season. As the construction of the East Stand gathered pace during that campaign, our fans could see a very visual sign of a major step forward for Barnsley Football Club. They were finally able to experience the comforts on offer on 6 March 1993, when we entertained Leicester City at Oakwell. Sadly, we were not able to commemorate the opening of the new stand with a victory, losing 3-2 to a late Gary Coatsworth winner. Inevitably, Coatsworth was a former Barnsley player who had come back to haunt us like so many others have done in the past. My most striking personal memory of that period, other than suffering an attack of vertigo when I was invited by the construction company to go to the very top of the development before the roof had been put on, was going up to Oakwell late on the Friday afternoon prior to the match against Leicester. As I walked across the pitch I have to confess to a tearful moment as I reflected on what had been achieved. The completion of the project was a proud moment for all connected with Barnsley Football Club and particular credit is due to Michael Spinks and John Kelly for overseeing the project, to the late Stuart Manley for his role as advisor to the Football Club, and to Peter Landon from the club's architects, Nuttall Yarwood, for their work on the project. The East Stand development cost £2.25million and was funded by a way of a £1.1million grant from the Football Trust with the balance coming from our own resources. The board believed that at an approximate cost of £350 per seat we were getting excellent value for money because our research had shown that many of our rivals were paying upwards of £500 per seat for their developments. The completion of this project was our first step on the way to compliance with the Taylor Report.

Following the influx of cash generated by the sales of Tiler and Agnew it meant that in addition to us being able to proceed with the East Stand development money was also available to the manager for strengthening the squad that summer and a number of players were brought in, notably goalkeeper Lee Butler (£160,000 from Aston Villa), Charlie Bishop (£50,000 from Bury), Gareth Williams (£150,000 from Aston Villa), Steve Davis (£180,000 from Crewe), Deiniol Graham (£50,000 from Manchester United) and John Pearson (£135,000 from Leeds United). Throughout my time as chairman, the board's policy on incoming transfers was generally that we would indicate to the manager the level of finance available for transfer fees and wages, but it was his decision on whom he wanted to sign. There were odd occasions when we were uncertain about his choices and John Pearson fell into that category. I had seen John a number of times over the years and told Mel that I thought he would be disappointed in him. Mel was determined to pursue the signing and John came to Oakwell from Leeds at a fee decided at tribunal of £130,000. Sadly, he suffered a serious neck injury that blighted his career at Barnsley. The other signing that caused much discussion amongst the board was Mel's wish early in the 1991-92 season to bring David Currie back to the club. David's stay at Nottingham Forest had been brief and he soon moved on to Oldham Athletic. After a poor start to the season Mel thought David would provide the creativity required to lift the team. However, David's return to the club didn't have the affect that Mel had hoped for. But, in the same week, Mel also agreed a deal with his good friend, Oldham boss Joe Royle, to bring Neil Redfearn in on loan. Neil was unsettled at Oldham because, although he had played a big part in the success that Oldham were having at the time, Royle felt that he was better suited on the right-hand side of midfield, but Neil preferred a more central role. He initially came for a month, and so impressed Mel that he recommended to the board that we try and sign him permanently. We agreed a fee with Oldham for £180,000, but Neil proved to be a very stubborn negotiator. We met him and his then advisor, former Leeds United player Eddie Gray, in Mel's office on the Tuesday morning prior to a League Cup tie against Blackpool that evening. We were keen to tie up a deal so that Neil could play that night but it didn't happen. Neil ignored his advisor and the exhortations from myself and Mel and left Oakwell still an Oldham player. We assumed that the deal was dead but later that week Neil had a change of heart and agreed to sign for Barnsley on the terms that had been offered him a few days earlier. To this day, I have no idea why Neil changed his mind, but I'm really pleased that he did. It turned out to be a great move for Barnsley Football Club and a great move for Neil Redfearn who, over the years, was recognised by Barnsley fans as a true Oakwell hero. So highly is he still regarded by those Reds fans he was recently voted their all-time favourite player. Neil often says he broke the unwritten footballer's rule of never falling in love with his employers when his love affair with Barnsley Football Club started. But neither he, nor anybody else, could have predicted what was going to happen when he signed that contract in October 1991.

In spite of the influx of players for the 1991-92 season, we finished in a disappointing sixteenth place, neither flirting with relegation nor challenging for the top spots. At the end of that season, Mel's first team player-coach John Deehan left the club because he was unable to accept the reduced terms offered when he hung up his boots, and he was replaced by the Barnsley-born Mick Wadsworth. I had got to know Mick in my early days as a director when he was helping Bobby Collins with the juniors on a part-time basis. In the intervening years, Mick had earned a great reputation in his role as FA Regional Coach for the North West. Mel had also got to know Mick from his time at Manchester City so it seemed an ideal appointment. The 1992-93 season started in disappointing fashion, with the first nine games yielding only a solitary win and two draws. Once again Mel felt that we needed to freshen things up and recommended the signing of Wayne Biggins from Stoke City. 'Bertie', as he was known, scored on his debut at Leicester City and then got two more the following week in a 3-0 home win over Luton Town. We had been unable to agree a fee with Stoke City for Biggins and after much discussion between myself and my counterpart at Stoke, Peter Coates, the fee was eventually fixed by tribunal at £200,000. Although results improved and we were to finish thirteenth in the table, attendances were starting to dwindle and incredibly, we got less than 4,000 for a home game against Southend United during April. Our away form that season had been of particular concern, especially for the longer trips when the team had travelled the previous day. For our away trip to Millwall I suggested to Mel that he should deviate from the norm and treat the lads to a West End show on the night before the game. Mel, a very conservative man, thought that I was mad, but reluctantly agreed. The lads had a great night in the West End but Mel's mood wasn't improved when there was a problem with the team coach taking them back to the hotel at Waltham Abbey and they didn't get to bed until 2am. When I went to see the manager before the game his mood had clearly not improved but happily a 4-0 victory brought a rare smile to Mel's face.

My directors recognised before I did that the Mel Machin era had run out of steam and that a new face was required to freshen things up. Mel's last match as Barnsley manager was in a 3-1 defeat away at Brentford, after which I came to the same conclusion as the rest of my board. The work that Mel Machin did at Barnsley Football Club and his personal pride and dignity demanded that his departure should be handled in a sensitive way. I had the unpleasant task of telling Mel that the board felt that we had reached the end of the road, but suggested to him that he may wish to tender his resignation on the understanding that the compensation clause detailed in his contract would be honoured by the club. I always believed that it was the job of a Football Club chairman to establish a strong working relationship with the manager and in Mel's case that was not difficult to do. It was an emotional day for me when Mel left Barnsley Football Club, but I'm glad to say that my wife and I have kept in touch with Mel and Jo over the years and we still remain on good terms. The Machin years provided stability at Barnsley Football Club and it's my belief that this stability played a part in future successes.

Following Mel's departure, Eric Winstanley was once again asked to take on the caretaker's role, assisted by First Team Coach Mick Wadsworth for the last match of the season against Swindon Town. However, the most crucial decision that was taken during their brief stint in charge of team affairs was to recommend to the board that the decision to release a young right-back named Nicky Eaden should be reversed. This recommendation was adopted and Nicky was given another contract. At the same time Chief Scout John Benson, who had been appointed by Mel, had been tracking a little midfielder at non-league Winsford United by the name of Darren Sheridan. John's recommendation was that we should sign him, but the board felt that this should be put on hold until a permanent manager was in position. The club continued to keep tabs on Sheridan though, and he was eventually signed the following season for £10,000. In spite of the reasonable final position in the league there was an air of gloom around Oakwell and the board and I felt the need to try and provide a spark.

CHAPTER 6

Two for the Price of One

W hen looking for a new manager, football clubs often appoint an individual whose character is diametrically opposite to that of his predecessor. And that certainly turned out to be the case at Barnsley Football Club in the summer of 1993. The vacant manager's position was advertised and we got the usual collection of applications. However, the football grapevine was buzzing with the fact that Leeds United's Gordon Strachan, whose contract at Elland Road was coming to an end that summer, was looking to move into management. The board felt that with his track record as a player and with his obvious leadership qualities, he would be an ideal appointment as player-manager at Oakwell. The directors and I discussed the situation at length and I was authorised to approach Gordon. Although this was technically contrary to FA regulations, I had a chat with him on the phone and he invited me to his home in north Leeds to talk further. At that first meeting Gordon was very impressive. Throughout his career he had been known as a dedicated professional and during our meeting it became clear that he was still passionate about football and was extremely ambitious. He and I seemed to get on very well and he confirmed that he was interested in the job at Barnsley. It was left that we'd each have a few days to think about things, but having reported back to the board they were unanimous in their view that Gordon Strachan would be the perfect man for Barnsley Football Club, so I arranged another meeting with Gordon at his home. The board and I knew that in order to tempt a highly-paid top Premiership player to come to Barnsley we would have to far outstrip the £60,000 per year that the previous manager had been paid. In the event I went to see Gordon for the second time and in response to a salary offer of £180,000, his reply, in a thick, Scottish accent, went something like: "Chairman, you're hardly spoiling me with money." Nonetheless, we shook hands on a deal with the only stumbling block being that Gordon had a pre-arranged meeting with the Leeds hierarchy of Howard Wilkinson, Bill Fotherby and Chairman Leslie Silver. We agreed that he'd ring me on the Friday evening of that week to confirm that he would not be signing a new contract at Elland Road and would be coming to Barnsley. Whilst I was delighted that we appeared to have our man, I was always conscious of the fact that if Leeds wanted him to stay, with their greater financial muscle they could blow us out of the water. When the phone didn't ring on the Friday I feared the worst, and when I eventually spoke to Gordon my doubts were confirmed. He was profusely apologetic, but a combination of far more money than we could ever offer him, a position on the coaching staff, as well as the belief that he still felt he had something to offer as a player at the highest level, combined to ensure that he would put his managerial ambitions on hold. By that stage in my career as a Football Club chairman, I had reached a point where I didn't get emotional about such dealings. This was business and Gordon made a business decision to stay at Leeds United. It was just one of those things and I have never had an axe to grind with Gordon Strachan.

However, the rejection had put us back to square one, but the board still felt that a big name with a lively personality was what we should be looking for. Although we received some very interesting applications including Paul Futcher, Ray McHale, a young Sam Allardyce, Dennis Smith, Brian Hamilton and Ian Porterfield, as well as a host of other names, we still fancied a big name manager and the next name to come into the frame was Viv Anderson, who had been at Sheffield Wednesday for a couple of years and prior to that had had what can only be described as a glittering career, first with Nottingham Forest, then Arsenal and then Manchester United. He had won everything with those clubs and was famously the first black player to be selected for England. Viv was out of contract at Sheffield Wednesday, having helped them to both cup finals the previous season. I contacted my counterpart at Hillsborough, Dave Richards, who is now Sir Dave Richards and Chairman of the FA Premier League. Describing Viv as a deep thinker about football and a great influence in the dressing room, his view was that it would be a great move for Barnsley and a great move for Viv. I rang Viv and arranged a meeting with him at the Cedar Court Hotel at Ainley Top, near Huddersfield. We had a long chat and he was very interested in coming to Barnsley. During our initial discussion, Viv made it plain that in spite of being thirty-seven years old he still thought he had a lot to offer as a player in the First Division, which was exactly what I wanted to hear. We talked about finance, and I agreed in principle that Barnsley Football Club would pay the same salary that he'd been getting at Hillsborough, around £100,000 per year.

It was while talking to Viv that what can either be described as a stroke of genius or a stroke of luck took place when I randomly remembered a conversation I'd had at that year's League Cup final with a member of Wednesday's coaching staff, Frank Barlow. Whilst walking away from Wembley Frank had given me insight into Wednesday midfielder Danny Wilson's character. Danny, who had played twenty times for Northern Ireland, was a quality player, a great passer of the ball and was fiercely determined. Like Viv his contract at Hillsborough was coming to an end, but even at thirty-three years of age, the coaching staff there were recommending to their board that Danny should get a new contract. Whilst chatting with Viv at the Cedar Court Hotel that day it struck me that Wilson and Anderson could make the perfect dream team for Barnsley. I suggested the possibility to Viv about bringing Danny in as his number two and he was really up for the idea. From the Football Club's point of view the major downside was that we'd have both the manager and assistant manager on the pitch at the same time, but with the experience of Eric Winstanley to assist them from the sidelines, I thought we had the perfect solution. The upside was that we were bringing in two top Premiership footballers with a wealth of experience in the game. After that initial meeting with Viv I reported back to the board, who were enthusiastic about the whole package, so at that stage I arranged a meeting for the three of us at a pub on the Derbyshire moors.

First impressions can often be deceptive, but that wasn't the case with Daniel Joseph Wilson. Danny came across as being bright, forthright, ambitious and was very interested in the possibility of being assistant manager to Viv at Barnsley. But Danny was never a pushover in contract negotiations, as I was to experience more than once in the future, and he made it clear from the outset that he wanted to be paid the same as his mate. Having reached an agreement with the pair, the arrangements were ratified by the Barnsley board and Viv Anderson and Danny Wilson joined Barnsley Football Club as manager and assistant manager respectively. We were delighted to have got our men, although I was disappointed with certain sections of the media who tried to focus on Viv's status as a black manager rather than simply accepting the fact that we had appointed a top footballer who hopefully was going to make a name for himself in management.

Viv came into the Oakwell hotseat and was indeed a lively and larger than life character who wore his heart on his sleeve. Danny's approach was much calmer and more considered than Viv's, and it was even suggested by some in the early days that we had got it the wrong way around. Nonetheless, there was a definite lifting of the spirits at Oakwell and we looked forward to the new season with relish. In addition to Anderson and Wilson joining the squad, the experienced Glynn Snodin and Sheffield United's Ian Bryson were also brought in. The season's opener was West Bromwich Albion at home, and although player-manager Anderson opened the scoring for Barnsley, the match ended with a 1-1 draw with the crowd of nearly 13,000 being very encouraging. The reign of Viv Anderson was like a rollercoaster for Barnsley Football Club. Sometimes we could be very good, and sometimes we were downright bad with an alarming habit of leaking goals. Viv had decided to move away from the three centre-half system that Mel Machin had adopted and went for a more traditional back four, with Gerry Taggart and Viv himself playing at centre-half. We lost 4-1 away at Peterborough in August and a week later also conceded four away at Middlesbrough. We then got thumped 5-0 at Luton Town in early October, but the final straw for me was an embarrassing 5-4 reverse at Stoke City later that month.

The policy of the board was always to provide the best possible environment in terms of finance and facilities for the manager, his coaching staff and his players. We did not believe that it was our job to get heavily involved in playing matters. But after the humiliation of the Stoke defeat, which saw us concede three own goals (two from Charlie Bishop and the other from Gary Fleming), I went against our own protocol and questioned Viv's team selection. In that conversation I made it clear to him that too many people had worked too hard over the years for Barnsley Football Club to see our First Division status put at risk in the name of his football principles. We were leaking too many goals, which in my opinion and in the opinion of the board, was as a direct result of him ditching the three centre half system favoured by Mel for his own flat back four preference. Viv was not best pleased by my intervention – understandably so – but soon afterwards he reverted to the three centre-half formation and that had the desired affect of tightening things up. A further concern was that the assistant manager was having a really difficult time on the field, to the point where he was taking a fair bit of stick from the Barnsley fans. Thankfully though, in true Danny Wilson fashion, he fought his way through that difficult early period and by the end of the season was a firm crowd favourite.

The first major signing of Viv's era was that of Andy Payton. Lou Macari had been appointed as manager of Celtic and made an offer to Viv for Wayne Biggins of £200,000. 'Bertie' had done well for Macari during their time together at Stoke. Viv turned down the offer and told me what he had done, as he and all other managers had a contractual obligation to inform the board of any approaches for our players. My view was that Biggins had had his best days at Barnsley and that the offer from Celtic was a good one. Viv's problem was that he didn't have many other striking options, so I suggested that he should offer

Macari a straight swap deal of Biggins for Payton. Andy had made his name as a goal scorer at Hull City, before moving to Middlesbrough for £900,000 with a similar valuation being placed on his head when he moved to Scotland. Viv didn't feel that Macari would take such a ludicrous offer seriously and didn't want to be embarrassed by the rejection from his old friend. I wasn't so sure because I had heard on the football grapevine that Payton had family issues and was looking to get back to England. I took the matter out of Viv's hands and spoke to Macari myself. Needless to say, he laughed out of court my original suggestion, but we eventually agreed a fee for Payton of £100,000 plus Wayne Biggins. I felt that was a good piece of business for Barnsley Football Club and when Payton and his representative, Stan Ternent, arrived at Oakwell for contract talks, we eventually agreed terms and he became our highest paid player at that time on a basic salary of just under £80,000 per year – a lot less money than he was earning at Celtic. Andy did well for the club, bagging forty-one goals in 108 appearances. Martin Bullock became Viv's next signing, coming from non-league outfit Eastwood Town for just £20,000. He'd been on our radar for some time and Viv invited him to play as a trialist in a reserve game against Oldham. This little scrap of a teenager, who only looked about twelve, was up against an experienced full-back, Andy Barlow. On a number of occasions early in the game, Bully picked up the ball and breezed past Barlow before the inevitable happened and he got clattered to the floor. Everyone in the crowd must have winced at the brutality of the challenge, but the young lad just bounced up and continued to torment Barlow for the rest of the game. At half time Viv and I had a quick chat and decided to ask Michael Spinks to get the paperwork sorted out so that we could sign Martin Bullock that night. Within half an hour of the game ending Bullock was a Barnsley player.

Our cup campaign that year began at non-league Bromsgrove Rovers where we were close to a humiliating defeat. Only very late goals from Andy Rammell and Owen Archdeacon saved us as we scraped through 2-1. The Barnsley performance that day had been an embarrassment and as I sat in my seat mentally preparing what I was going to say by way of congratulations to my counterpart from Bromsgrove and by way of explanation to the watching Sir Bert Millichip, then the Chairman of the Football Association, celebrity Barnsley fan Michael Parkinson and of course the media, I was reminded of two humiliating days in my father's era when cup ties were lost to non-league teams. The first was in 1970 against Rhyl, where after a replay at Oakwell, the tie was settled in Rhyl's favour 2-0 as just over 3,000 people rattled around the neutral venue of Old Trafford – how times change, you couldn't imagine a match of that insignificance being played at one of the major stadiums in the country these days. The second and most humiliating of all came some five years later as we crashed out of the cup at the first time of asking, 3-1 to Marine, a club based in the town of Crosby on the outskirts of Liverpool. The pain of this humiliation was etched on my father's face as he stood on the touchline watching his team being disgraced, and that afternoon at Bromsgrove I began to experience at first hand how he must have felt. To this day, as I do my usual Sunday morning scouring of football results at all levels, I still give a silent cheer if either Rhyl or Marine have lost the previous day. In the league the team continued to produce erratic results, and in early February I went to a meeting with Viv to point out to him that, with the run-in we had got from April until to the end of the season, we needed to pick up points pretty quickly. Fortunately, a run of nine games, which produced seven wins, convinced Viv that we had done enough to be safe, and he wasn't slow to tell me. But it wasn't until 30 April that our First Division status was assured when we beat Wolves 2-0 at Oakwell. The season stuttered to its end with the team finishing in eighteenth position, avoiding the drop by a mere four points. After the high hopes of the previous August this wasn't what the board had in mind, and the situation wasn't helped by some alarmingly low gates of less than 5,000 towards the latter part of the campaign.

Whatever misgivings the board might have had over Viv's position were heightened when I received a call out of the blue from Wolverhampton Wanderers Chairman Jonathan Hayward, the son of Sir Jack Hayward, the great Wolves benefactor. The board of Barnsley and particularly myself and Barry Taylor, had established a strong friendship with Sir Jack and his board, often jokingly telling him that he'd be more appreciated in Barnsley than at Wolves. It was common knowledge that Wolves had been in negotiations with the great Bryan Robson to take him to Molineux from Old Trafford as their player-manager. Jonathan thought he owed it to me to let me know that Robson had requested that Viv Anderson should join him as his number two. Apparently, Viv and Bryan had reached an understanding when they were at Manchester United together that if and when Bryan became a manager, he would invite Viv to join him as his right hand man. The talks between Robson and Wolves collapsed, but with the revelation that our manager was actively being linked with other jobs, it did make me wonder how great his commitment really was to Barnsley. Sure enough, a few weeks later Robson agreed terms to become player-manager at Middlesbrough. Soon after that Viv called me to ask for permission to speak to 'Boro. I made it clear to him that before he did so Barnsley would need concrete assurances about compensation as clearly outlined in his contract. I think he was rather taken aback but I have no doubt that if the boot had been on the other foot and Viv had been sacked he would have been reminding me of the terms of the contract. Later that day I received a call from 'Boro's Chief Executive Keith Lamb, and he half-heartedly tried to negotiate a better deal for them. But Keith knew the score and we ended up getting our compensation. I was a little bit surprised that a guy who was a manager in his own right would settle for being a number two to somebody else, but if that's what he wanted to do then I certainly wasn't going to stand in his way.

Once again we were managerless, and although there was a flurry of interest in the job, the board felt that in Danny Wilson we had a natural successor without causing too much disruption to the club. The vice-chairman and I met with Danny to gauge his interest and he made it very clear that he wanted the job in spite of the fact that we had told him that we weren't in a position to improve his contract nor was it likely that if money became available through the selling of players that he would see very much of it because the club was under pressure to progress the development of the stadium in an attempt to comply with the Taylor Report. In his year as assistant to Viv, Danny had made a massive impression on everybody at the Football Club, especially the board, and when Barry and I reported back on our talks with Wilson the board unanimously agreed to give Wilson the job. The rest, as they say, is history.

CHAPTER 7

Oh Danny Boy

It was sod's law that we finished sixth in Danny Wilson's debut season as manager of Barnsley Football Club in 1994-95. At the end of that campaign the Premier League was due to reduce from twenty-two to twenty clubs, the implication being that only two teams were to be promoted from Division One with four coming down from the top flight. In any other season a sixth place finish would have guaranteed a play-off spot, but sadly not in this particular campaign. So, despite a very good season, the club was not rewarded with a shot at the big time. The excellent performances demonstrated to the fans that in Danny Wilson, we seemed to have made the right choice. He himself had led from the front on the field, being voted as the fans' Player of the Year and off the field he was the runner-up in the Football League Manager of the Year awards. With young players such as David Watson, Nicky Eaden and Andy Liddell making themselves regulars in the team, and with Darren Sheridan doing likewise, the future looked bright at Oakwell despite the average crowd for the season being as low as 6,508 for league games. Nonetheless, a sixth place finish was still our highest position for a number of years so on the back of that there were high hopes for the following season.

The second phase of the stadium development had been completed with the building of the new South Stand – the Ponty End to all true Barnsley fans. The £2million development, aided by a £1.05million grant from the Football Trust, a £200,000 interest free loan from the Football Trust and a £700,000 loan from NatWest, the majority of which needed to be repaid within twelve months, consisted of 5,000 seats and included the club's main administration block and the Reds superstore. Barnsley-born Malcolm Hanson, a successful businessman based in Berkshire who ran an electronics company named ORA, agreed a deal to become both shirt sponsor and sponsor of the new stand. The name of ORA became synonymous with the old Ponty End in particular and Barnsley Football Club in general. As that development was taking shape the club also decided, as a stopgap measure, to put seating on the open terraces of the Spion Kop and in the lower tier of the West Stand. When this work had been finalised it meant that, miraculously, we had somehow managed to conform to the demands of the Taylor Report whilst at the same time giving us an overall seated capacity of 18,500. Little were we to know how soon in the future all of that capacity would be required.

In the summer of 1995, crowd favourite Gerry Taggart was sold to Bolton Wanderers for a total fee of £1.5million although fifty per cent of the profit on the original fee was due to Manchester City, such a high percentage reflecting the initial low price that we had paid for a player of such huge potential. Gerry wasn't adequately replaced until early November when Dutchman Arjan de Zeeuw joined the Barnsley ranks. The deal to sign Arjan was a tortuous one, perhaps the most difficult contract talks in which I was ever involved. A fee had been agreed with Dutch club Telstar of £188,000, so Arjan flew to England along with his agent, Humphrey Neuman, and his father-in-law to try and finalise contract terms. The negotiations took place in one of the executive boxes in the East Stand on the Thursday morning, but hours of bickering, arguments and hassle soon followed. In any contract negotiations my preference was always to discuss terms with the agent alone because it was a purely business discussion, whereas sometimes players would tend to get a little emotional. When Humphrey listed his and Arjan's expectations I realised it was going to be a long day. The numbers that they were talking about were way out of our league, and when I revealed that our top paid player was on £78,000 and that we were prepared to match that for Arjan's signature, they threatened to walk out and fly back to Holland. Even at that early stage I would have gladly driven them back to Manchester Airport myself, but

Danny and Michael Spinks, who were both present, calmed me down. After protracted exchanges we finally came up with an offer to make Arjan our first £100,000 per year player, and we sensed that he and his father-in-law were satisfied with that. Sadly, our friend Humphrey was like little Oliver Twist and kept asking for more. I'd just about had enough and felt that a frank discussion between the two of us on our own would get the point across to Humphrey that we had gone as far as we were going. I invited him into another executive box and when I had made mine and the club's position very clear in blunt terms, Humphrey finally got the message and I suspect that the very forthright way that I spoke to him will have extended his knowledge of the English language quite dramatically. Following that 'conversation' he recommended to his player that he should sign for Barnsley on the proposed terms. I then left Oakwell, leaving Michael Spinks to prepare the contract, and he had the dubious pleasure of Humphrey hovering over his shoulder as this process was completed. Arjan made his debut on the following Saturday against Wolves at Oakwell and after a shaky first twenty minutes began to show the qualities that persuaded Danny to sign him in the first place. Humphrey and I had many conversations in the years to come, usually concerning Arjan de Zeeuw, although he did once offer us another of his clients, Jimmy Floyd Hasselbaink, who then went on to sign for Leeds United. Obviously Jimmy would have made a great signing, but the initial transfer fee alone was way beyond our means.

The feel good factor surrounding Oakwell at the start of the 1995-96 season had started to ebb away, as mixed results left the team becalmed in mid-table for most of the campaign. The season wasn't without incident, however, and having drawn Arsenal at home in the Coca-Cola Cup after overcoming the old enemy Huddersfield Town 4-2 in the first round, we were all relishing the prospect of a great night against the mighty Arsenal at Oakwell. Sadly, the match was lost 3-0, but the evening was overshadowed by racial abuse aimed at Ian Wright by a section of the Barnsley fans. Whilst I was, and remain sure, that this foul-mouthed minority did not truly represent the vast body of Barnsley supporters, nonetheless it was left to the board and I to attempt to restore the good name of Barnsley Football Club. There was a storm of media interest in the situation but I felt that a low-key approach dealing directly with Arsenal away from the glare of the media spotlight would be the best way to deal with the matter. I contacted Arsenal Vice-Chairman David Dein, someone who by that stage in my career as chairman I'd got to know reasonably well, to personally apologise to him. I also wrote directly to Ian Wright on behalf of Barnsley Football Club. Ian duly rang me to thank me for the way the matter had been handled by Barnsley and the issue was laid to rest. Another cup controversy that season took place at Boundary Park, Oldham in an FA third round replay. The worst ever penalty decision in history was given against Owen Archdeacon that night by referee George Cain for a supposed trip by Archdeacon on Oldham fans' favourite Gunnar Halle. Sitting in my seat in the directors' box, I was nearer to Halle than Archdeacon was when Halle went down, but the referee still gave the spot-kick and we lost 2-1. In point of fact, it was a second awful decision that Cain had made surrounding that cup tie because the previous Tuesday night he had actually postponed the match half an hour before kick-off due to fog, but by 7.45pm the evening was as clear as a bell.

In addition to the signature of Arjan de Zeeuw, Peter Shirtliff had previously joined the club, with Danny bringing in Liverpool great Jan Molby on a month's loan. Although Jan had always been a great passer of the ball, he was never the most mobile, and by that stage of his career he'd lost a further yard of pace. However, an incident occurred prior to our home match against Leicester City in early October which, although made me smile, was a bit harsh on Jan. Before the match I had been loitering near the dugout waiting to receive a presentation on the pitch from local artist Suzanne Myers, and after a few moments the visiting Leicester fans, who were then accommodated to the left of the players' tunnel, spotted the rather bulky frame of the Barnsley chairman and started singing: "Is it Molby? Is it Molby? Is it Molby in a suit?" I never had the heart to tell Jan at the time, but I do know that some years later a close friend of mine, John Hepworth, met Jan at a dinner and regaled him with the tale. A further change took place in the February of that season when former Manchester United striker Andy Rammell left to join Southend United for £185,000. As part of the deal to take him to Southend, Danny agreed to sign striker Dave Regis for £50,000. Dave is the brother of Cyrille, the cousin of sprinter John Regis and uncle to Jason Roberts. He was a smashing lad, but didn't have the best of times at Oakwell. He is best remembered by Barnsley fans for a sitter he missed in front of the Spion Kop at Oakwell against Grimsby Town. Folklore has it that he was on the goal line when he mis-kicked, but having recently viewed the footage I'm pleased to confirm that he was actually 3 feet from goal when he sliced his shot wide.

As the season slithered away Danny asked to see me in order to talk about the future direction of the club. He was concerned that many of the more experienced players had probably given their best days to Barnsley Football Club and he felt that radical changes needed to be made that summer. He identified a number of players who fell into this category and at the next board meeting Danny's views were considered by the directors who unanimously agreed to back the manager. Significantly, the Football League were in negotiations with Sky Television for a proper televised football rights contract and the early indications were that it was likely that an average First Division club would receive £750,000 per year as opposed to the peanuts that we were getting from ITV for their goals highlights package. To put this into perspective, Barnsley Football Club's total annual turnover for the financial year of 1995/96 was something in the region of £2million, so the impact of this potential deal was huge. It would give us the opportunity to back Danny regardless of player sales, both in terms of transfer fees and player wages. After the high hopes leading into the season, our tenth placed finish seemed disappointing, but our focus rapidly turned to the work that was going to be done that summer to re-shape the squad. Not even in my wildest dreams could I have predicted the events of the following season.

CHAPTER 8

It's Just Like Watching Brazil

It's very rare that a football club manager can ever boast of a 100 per cent success rate in the transfer market, but that's precisely what Danny Wilson could claim about the five players that came to Oakwell in the summer of 1996. We had already decided that a number of players needed to be sold, and the first of those to leave the Football Club was Andy Payton. Early in the summer I agreed a deal with the then Huddersfield Town Chairman Malcolm Asquith for Andy to move to West Yorkshire for £312,500. The Huddersfield board, in those days, bizarrely used to rotate their chairman every two years, but this wasn't an idea that I was particularly fond of and thankfully neither were any of my directors. Owen Archdeacon soon departed to Carlisle United for £30,000, Charlie Bishop went to Wigan Athletic for £40,000, with Lee Butler being released on a free transfer. The manager himself raised a further £125,000 with the sale of midfielder Brendan O'Connell to Charlton Athletic, and Gary Fleming retired from the game due to a serious knee injury. One of the players that we did not want to leave Oakwell was club Captain Neil Redfearn. Towards the end of the previous season there had been much media speculation suggesting that Redfearn was looking for a new club, but the manager and I felt that Neil still had much to offer. His goals alone would have been difficult to replace, but with all the other comings and goings that we were anticipating that summer we felt that Neil's departure would send out the wrong message to the fans. Neil and

Danny met to discuss a new contract for the player, and with terms agreed between the two of them the manager's recommendations were accepted by the board. With Danny himself having agreed an extended contract towards the end of the previous season, the two most inspirational figures at the club had now committed their futures to Barnsley.

Boosted by the confirmation that Sky TV had indeed committed themselves to a £25million per year package with the Football League, we were then in a good position to start bringing in new faces. The first summer signing was left-back Neil Thompson, who had been released by Ipswich Town on a free transfer. Danny had been made aware of Thompson's availability and was very keen to sign him. He suggested that I should ring Ipswich Chairman David Sheepshanks, who I had known for many years, to find out what the position was. David reassured me about Thompson's fitness, but said that he was aware that Neil was going for talks with Leyton Orient the following day. I asked him to do me the favour of speaking to Neil to tell him of Barnsley's interest and to put on hold his discussions with Orient. Neil agreed to do this and after speaking to Danny he became a Barnsley player. Matty Appleby was soon brought on board. The former Newcastle youngster had made his name in the lower leagues with Darlington and Danny was convinced he could make the step up. A fee was agreed with Darlington of £150,000, with further incentive payments agreed at £30,000. Veteran striker Paul Wilkinson became Danny's next target and his interest was heightened by the fact that, surprisingly, Middlesbrough were prepared to release him on a free transfer. Paul's career had begun at Grimsby and taken him to Watford, Everton and Middlesbrough, but when 'Boro hit the big time, bringing in foreign stars such as Ravanelli, Wilkinson became surplus to requirements. The previous season he'd had loan spells at Luton Town and then Watford, who were keen to sign him permanently but couldn't meet 'Boro's asking price of £750,000. Protracted negotiations between Paul's agent and myself were successfully concluded with Wilkinson coming to Oakwell as the club's highest paid player on approximately £150,000 per year. Danny's next move, literally, took him to Portugal, as little Clint Marcelle joined the club from Portuguese side FC Felgueiras. The legendary Sir Bobby Robson, at that time manager of FC Porto, had recommended Clint to Ipswich chief scout Charlie Woods. Ipswich were well served with wingers at the time so Charlie recommended Clint to his good friend Eric Winstanley, Danny's first team coach. Clint was in dispute with his club for the not so insignificant reason that they hadn't been paying his wages, so that fact meant that he was available for transfer for a nominal fee. I had many conversations with his agent Alex Kristic who, in turn, was dealing with the FC Felgueiras chairman. He seemed to move the goalposts on the deal every day so by the time the saga had dragged on for nearly three weeks, I suggested to Danny that he and Assistant Club Secretary Chris Patzelt should fly out to Portugal so that he could sort the deal out face-to-face, or bin it. I'd already provisionally agreed terms with Clint's agent and happily Danny and Chris overcame all of the obstacles as they agreed terms to pay a transfer fee of £35,000 for Clint. Whilst Danny was in Europe, Clint's agent recommended to him another one of his clients, Serbian midfielder Jovo Bosancic, who was also plying his trade in Portugal but was available on a free transfer. Danny invited Jovo to come to Oakwell for a trial and with some trepidation decided to take a chance on him. Our aim that summer had been to get the squad sorted out as quickly as possible so that Danny had the opportunity of having a full pre-season with his new look squad. From a personal point of view it meant that I could get away for a much-needed family holiday before the season started, although I always kept in touch with Oakwell whenever I was away.

The season's opener was at the Hawthorns, the scene of seriously bad memories for me. I was really looking forward to seeing the new look Barnsley team in action for the first time, having missed most of the pre-season friendlies. I couldn't believe how well we started the game. Clint Marcelle gave us the lead before West Brom equalised from the penalty spot after a Matty Appleby handball. However, Andy Liddell's winner gave us a much-merited first win of the season. The next four games saw the team produce more of the same with, for me, the most memorable of these victories being at Maine Road where a Clint Marcelle double saw us beat Manchester City. The final game in that sequence was a 3-0 thrashing of Stoke City at Oakwell, with a Neil Thompson screamer from 30 yards being one of many memorable goals we scored that season. Unbeaten, with a perfect winning start at the top of the league, there was a real belief, both inside Oakwell and amongst the faithful, that we could be serious promotion contenders. However, we had sold less than 2,500 season tickets and although attendances were better, we still had some convincing to do in the town that we really meant business. For many years the club had struggled to dispel the view that there was no ambition and we clearly still had work to do to convince people otherwise. I must hasten to add that then and throughout all of my time as chairman of Barnsley Football Club, I was always grateful to those fans who did pay their hard-earned money to come and watch the team and that season particularly they were getting a real treat. The matchday atmosphere at Oakwell in the early days of the promotion season was excellent and was enhanced by the now famous 'It's just like watching Brazil' song that would echo around the Oakwell stands. That chant became our trademark that season and beyond, and it still brings a smile to my face and a shiver down my spine whenever I hear it today.

The good form continued and in October the board and I agreed to offer Danny support should he wish to further strengthen the squad. We had shown a surplus in our transfer dealings that summer and, of course, the enhanced TV money further improved our financial position. During the summer Danny had made an inquiry for Middlesbrough's Scottish forward John Hendrie, who had been a deadly foil for Paul Wilkinson at 'Boro. Danny's old friend Viv had quoted him £1million, so Danny hadn't pursued it. We agreed that Danny should make contact with Viv again and he was informed that £500,000 would do the deal. The next step was for me to speak to my old friend Keith Lamb, the 'Boro chief executive, who confirmed that they would take £500,000. My opening gambit was that we didn't have that sort of money and that we'd take him on a free transfer to get him off of their wage bill. When Keith had stopped laughing we finally managed a sensible conversation, and a fee was agreed of £250,000, with £100,000 being paid up front, £100,000 the following August and £50,000 the August after that (the significance of the August date being that that is the month when clubs receive the bulk of their television money). John's terms were similar to those of Paul Wilkinson – less money than he was on at Middlesbrough – and he made his debut as a second-half substitute in a 0-0 draw against Crystal Palace. He was clearly short of match fitness but by the end of the month he'd scored his first goal for the Reds in a 3-1 away win at Port Vale, striking a beauty with the outside of his right foot from the edge of the box. John was up and running and went on to score fifteen goals that season. We carried on our merry way, impressing the football world with our free-flowing style. But a seminal moment for me was the 1-0 win against Sheffield United at Bramall Lane four days before Christmas, with Hendrie's winner sending us to the top of the league.

Despite all the changes made to the squad the team had knitted remarkably well. Goalkeeper David Watson had been a regular for the England Under 21 squad for some time and was surely destined for full international honours. He was a Barnsley lad who loved the Football Club, and it was a tragedy that his career ended prematurely a few years later due to injury. Arjan de Zeeuw had developed into one of the best centre-halves in the league and his partner, Steve Davis, was playing the best football of his Barnsley career until a bad tackle against Queens Park Rangers in January broke his leg and ended his season. Our involvement in the FA Cup ended a fortnight later on the same ground, when we lost 3-2 in a match that featured a wonder strike, an overhead scissor kick by Rangers striker Trevor Sinclair. I must confess that I still feel sick whenever I see it replayed on television. With Davis's injury, a young Adie Moses was given an opportunity and with his pace and technique proved an able replacement. Matty Appleby was a revelation in the sweeper's role, proving to be a great reader of the game and a good passer of the ball. The experience that Peter Shirtliff had gained throughout his long career proved invaluable on occasions, and the two wing-backs, Nicky

Eaden and Neil Thompson, served the team admirably both defensively and going forward. I always felt that Nicky was undervalued by the Barnsley fans and his hard work up and down that right flank, coupled with a phenomenal ability to cross the ball, would earn him a place if ever I were to select my all-time favourite Barnsley XI.

The midfield was dominated by Neil Redfearn, who was playing, arguably, the best football of his career. His goals were invaluable and he proved to be an inspirational skipper. Partnering him was Darren 'Stumpy' Sheridan, who was a tough little so-and-so with a great left foot who knew how to look after himself and his mates. He had been brought up in the Moss Side area of Manchester and had joined the ranks of professional football with Barnsley at a relatively late age. He was one of the livelier characters in the dressing room, although many of his jokes and pranks have to be deemed X-rated. One little tale that can be told came one warm summer's afternoon when John Kelly and I had arrived at Oakwell for a board meeting, resplendent in our dark suits and sunglasses. As Sheridan walked passed I heard him say in a loud stage whisper to his mate: "My God, I didn't know we'd got the Blues Brothers on the board at this Football Club." Jovo Bosancic had a mercurial spirit and was another lively character. Clearly, the less structured way that football was run on the continent had rubbed off on Jovo because whenever I went in the dressing room after a victory to congratulate the players, Jovo would buttonhole me and exclaim: "Mr President, you come with cash bonus?" On every occasion Jovo was to be disappointed. Clint Marcelle proved to be a revelation with his pace and ability to beat a man. His goals that season were also invaluable and his very cosmopolitan background made him an unusual addition to the Oakwell staff. Many of Martin Bullock's cameo appearances from the bench were also vital, with his pace and inventiveness causing untold problems to tired defenders late on in games. Up front the veteran partnership of Wilkinson and Hendrie carried on where they left off at Middlesbrough, scoring goals and making chances for others. Although neither of them were in their first flush of youth they were still top players, and it's my belief that in the case of Wilkinson, he reproduced the kind of form that had made him a top-flight footballer. He may not have always been the easiest on the eye, but he gave his all for Barnsley Football Club that season. John Hendrie had always been a very clever footballer and the experience and know-how of the pair of them were important in our success that season. Andy Liddell was another important member of the squad, chipping in with eight goals.

Although the team never dropped below fourth in the table all season, it wasn't until the turn of the year that attendances consistently improved. As late as November we had a home crowd of just 7,500 for the 3-2 win over Portsmouth, but from the New Year onwards crowds grew as more fans started to believe in the impossible dream, and by the end of the season we had an average attendance of 11,356 for league games. One of the more quirky aspects to the season was the bitter rivalry with fellow promotion hopefuls Wolverhampton Wanderers. This rivalry was stoked by some unfortunate remarks by their manager, Mark McGhee, to the media. McGhee really upset the Oakwell faithful when he said that the Premier League would prefer Wolves to be promoted rather than Barnsley, simply because they were a 'big club'. I suspect that in reality Mark's comments may well have been taken out of context, but it was disappointing that an experienced manager should put himself in that situation. Our fans responded in typically humorous fashion with Mark McGhee becoming public enemy number one at Oakwell. The words to The Monkees' 'Sleepy Jean' song were adapted to be as insulting as possible to Mark McGhee, and whilst I wouldn't want to reproduce them here I have fond memories of 10,000 Barnsley fans soaked to the skin outside the Town Hall singing the re-arranged lyrics in mocking tribute to McGhee. The song was very catchy and I often found myself muttering it under my breath. McGhee's words provided something of a focal point for our fans and Danny would often use them in his pre-match team talks.

As the season progressed the tension grew and it became clear that we were in for a nail-biting finish. Bolton looked to be running away with the title and as we entered the home straight, the second automatic promotion spot was going to be a contest between Barnsley and Wolves. On the Tuesday night ahead of the Bradford City game on the Saturday we had a re-arranged fixture at Fratton Park to take on Portsmouth. I made the long drive to the south coast and was accompanied in my car by Michael Spinks and three of my colleagues from the board, John Kelly, Ian Potter and Chris Harrison. Our promotion hopes suffered a major setback that night as we lost the game 4-2. Neil Redfearn scored both of our goals with Lee Bradbury notching a hat-trick for the home side. The journey back to Barnsley was a long and sombre one because the general feeling in the car was that it was advantage Wolves. They were at home to Grimsby Town the following evening and it was difficult to imagine that they'd slip up. It had been my intention not to attempt to follow their progress but to simply get the final score at the end of the game. However, both my daughters decided otherwise and when they told me that Grimsby had equalised just before half-time I spent the next hour glued to Ceefax. Grimsby hung on for their 1-1 draw, which meant that the situation was crystal clear – if we beat Bradford City at Oakwell on that Saturday of 26 April 1997, we would be promoted to the Premier League.

From that Thursday, the expectation and the tension in the town became almost tangible, but the only person that I knew who appeared untouched by it was Danny Wilson. He went about his business in his usual calm and controlled manner and if he was feeling the pressure, it certainly didn't show as he prepared his squad for what was to be one of the biggest day in Barnsley's history. When the Saturday came around I had decided to adhere to my normal matchday routine, arriving at Oakwell with my family at about 1.45pm. The crowd was beginning to build by that stage and in the boardroom we were pleased to entertain many local dignitaries and other long-terms fans such as Dickie Bird and Michael Parkinson. In fact, at the end of the game when the pair were posing for photographs, my elder daughter very kindly offered Parky use of her Barnsley scarf, which he duly accepted. I have to confess to extreme nerves prior to the game and although I was always nervous before every match this one was exceptional. As chairman part of my duties was to entertain visiting directors in the boardroom, but I found it difficult at the best of times to indulge in small talk as kick-off time approached and often would disappear for ten minutes to try and calm myself down. Wilko's opener after twenty minutes temporarily eased my nerves, if not anyone else's, but it was only Clint's decider, with five minutes left on the clock, when I could start to enjoy the day. For the first time in the club's history we had made it into the top-flight – and the Football Club and the town began to party. It was the greatest achievement the club had ever seen and Danny, his backroom staff and his players deserved their glory. Star player John Hendrie, in an article in the *Sunday Times* in 2011, confessed that of all the highlights of his long career gaining promotion to the Premier League with Barnsley was the greatest of them. Having spoken to many of the players since those days they all felt the same as John.

The following day I'd got an appalling hangover but was committed to doing an early morning interview with Radio Five Live. Throughout the day I had numerous very touching phone calls from friends, colleagues and acquaintances offering their congratulations as the whole day passed in a blur. On the Monday I was committed to sitting on a Football League tribunal hearing at the League's headquarters at Lytham St Annes, which was investigating a dispute between Leicester City and our old friends at Wolves (ironically, I was the Wolves appointee to that tribunal). I have to say I didn't want to be there, I wanted to be in my proper place in Barnsley but was unable to get out of that particular commitment. My wife bought every newspaper that she possibly could and I got great pleasure from reading the accolades to Barnsley Football Club. Although I felt an overwhelming sense of tiredness after the rollercoaster of the previous few weeks, I knew that the following day was the start of our preparations for the Premiership. The season wasn't quite over because we still had the final fixture at Oxford United on the Sunday, and I was looking forward to the lads signing off in style. That they did, but not in the way that I was hoping for, getting hammered 5-1. Hammered seems to be the most appropriate word I can use for that performance because I suspect that that's what most of the players had been that week.

The season was over, the dream had come true and for the first time in 110 years Barnsley Football Club would take its place in the top division of English football. Over the years I have been asked many times to explain how little old Barnsley made it to the Premier League. It's simple – we had a very good manager and a very good first team coach who had assembled a squad of very good players with a great blend of youth and experience. Those players bought into the vision of the manager who made it clear to each of them what their role in the team would be. Promotion was achieved with what was one of the lowest budgets in the league that season of £2.5million for all employees at the club. I also believe that the platform that had been laid down at Barnsley Football Club was due to the hard work and vision of previous Boards of Directors and managers. Additionally, the Sky TV deal had at last given us the opportunity to compete on a more equal footing with other so-called bigger clubs. We also had one of the best administrators in the game in our General Manager, Michael Spinks, whose off the field team were dedicated to the football club. The board of the time was made up of relatively young, energetic local businessmen who were Barnsley fans through and through. We all worked hard in our own ways to contribute to the club's success and my earlier vision of seeing Barnsley Football Club as a well-respected member of the football establishment had been achieved. All of these factors, and many more, were responsible for the club's achievement. Of course, Danny Wilson was the inspiration and driving force of this success and was rightly recognised by his peers for what he had achieved by voting him Managers' Manager of the Year.

CHAPTER 9

We are Premier League

T he task of competing in the world's best and most financially driven football league was huge – both on and off the field. Behind the scenes changes needed to be made to Oakwell to accommodate the expected flock of media personnel who were likely to visit the club the following season. For that purpose a section of the West Stand behind the visiting directors' box was converted into a new and modern press facility. At the same time we increased the capacity of the visiting directors' box, again with the purpose of accommodating increased numbers of guests. The old office block behind the West Stand was converted into a press room so that journalists had space to work and where press conferences could be held after games by managers, players and other officials. Previously interviews had been conducted in the corridor outside the boardroom in the West Stand because the press room, such as it was, was not much bigger than a cupboard. We were painfully aware that both the home and away dressing rooms were clearly inadequate to host Premier League teams, the away dressing room in particular. Unfortunately we had very little scope to make improvements other than minor cosmetic changes. To compound matters further, the away dressing room was situated above the boiler room, so even on the chilliest of Oakwell days the away dressing room was like a furnace. This was not to go down well with many of our elite opponents, but I was regularly assured during the season that there was nothing that could be done about it. It was further decided that improvements needed to be made to the boardroom and this was the one and only occasion in my near twenty years on the board that any money was spent on directors' facilities. The room was refurbished with new oak panelling and was extended by knocking through into what was the ladies' guests room. It seems very strange reading those words and by way of background I need to explain that up until then the boardroom at Oakwell was strictly an all-male enclave, with directors' wives and female guests being expected to use the adjacent ladies' room. It is to my and my board's eternal shame that we allowed this situation to continue until as recently as 1997. By that stage it had become untenable to have such an archaic arrangement, and on more than one occasion it caused embarrassment as well as a certain amount of humour. When football started seeing the first female executives entering the industry our rule had to be relaxed to allow women executives to mingle in the main boardroom. Unsurprisingly this used to be a particularly sore point with our own wives, particularly when the visiting executives were of the younger and more nubile type such as Karren Brady. In fact, a couple of years before the changes were made we had a little bit of an incident with the then Chief Executive of the FA, Graham Kelly, and his partner, who arrived as our guests to watch a game and were shocked when it was suggested that Graham should come into the boardroom and his partner should be entertained in the ladies' room. Graham, with good humour, made a point of spending the afternoon in the ladies' room rather than the boardroom, and very pointedly wrote to my wife to thank her for her hospitality that afternoon, suggesting that he'd had more fun where he had been rather than with dull as dishwater football club directors. It was widely accepted in football that the boardroom hospitality at Barnsley Football Club was amongst the best in the country. Not that we provided particularly fine dining – our speciality was meat and potato pie, chips and peas – but rather that for many years we had always provided our guests with a very warm welcome. From our point of view, having the opportunity to meet our counterparts from other clubs as well as visiting dignitaries from the football authorities gave us the chance to discuss the issues of the day, to learn about other clubs and the issues that they faced and also to get to know people with whom we might be doing business in the future.

Our planning for the Premiership had actually started well before promotion was confirmed, not because we were taking promotion for granted, nor did we wish to tempt fate, but in the normal course of running the business each year our plans for the following season had already been worked on well before the end of the previous season. On this occasion we had two sets of plans, either of which we could have actioned depending upon the outcome of the season. We had done financial forecasts based on projected season ticket sales, visiting fan numbers, commercial revenues, and had spoken to the Premier League to ascertain what funds we might expect from their television and other commercial arrangements. This information gave us a good idea of what funds could be made available to Danny Wilson to strengthen the playing staff. The unanimous view of the board was that our fantastic fans, who had supported the club in ever-growing numbers during the promotion season, deserved and expected to see as much investment as possible in the squad.

Barnsley folk will fondly remember the buzz around the Football Club and the town that summer. Season tickets were much sought after and eager fans camped out through the night in the Oakwell car park to make sure that they got the seat of their choice. To put it mildly, no matter what planning had been done to deal with this unprecedented demand, nothing could quite prepare us for the avalanche of interest. To put things into perspective, the club had sold less than 2,500 full season tickets throughout the previous summer but following promotion 16,000 were snapped up within a couple of weeks. It was all hands to the pump for everyone at Oakwell that summer, with many of our loyal staff working long, long days. Their effort was outstanding, but so also was the patience and good humour of our supporters. I believe that anyone who wanted a season ticket that summer got one and although we had a further ground capacity after season ticket sales, of around 2,500, most of that capacity was reserved for away supporters on the open Kop end, with just a few hundred tickets available for home fans who hadn't bought season tickets. All of this meant that Oakwell would be packed to the rafters for virtually every game – a prospect almost unimaginable to those like myself who had followed Barnsley through the dark days of the 1960s. Net revenue after VAT from season tickets sales brought in just over £3million and we were led to believe that we could expect payments from the Premier League in the region of £5million. Throughout the season the Premier League would deposit sums of money into our bank account, which they quaintly referred to as 'bits and bobs'. These 'bits and bobs' could be as much as £100,000, and whilst to them it might have been loose change, for us it was manna from heaven.

Barnsley Football Club was officially confirmed as a member of the FA Premier League on Thursday 5 June 1997, at the Premier League's Annual General Meeting. This meeting formed part of the Premier League Chairman's Conference, held at the plush Ettington Park Hotel near Stratford-upon-Avon in the Warwickshire countryside. Michael Spinks and I were invited to represent the club, and I think it's worth making the point that by that stage in my football career, Michael and I, as well as Barry Taylor, were reasonably well known in football circles. I had been Barnsley's chairman since 1989 and a director since 1984, Barry having joined the board at the same time as myself, becoming an FA councillor since 1990. Michael had been the club secretary for twenty years, having been appointed by my father in the late 1970s. Michael and I arrived at the Chairman's Conference to take coffee with our fellow attendees on the lawn at 11am, and although we were slightly patronised by one chairman, who expressed the hope that we would enjoy our 'season' in the top flight, everyone else was extremely welcoming and hospitable. Following our introductory cup of coffee we adjourned to the conference room for a long and informative business session. This was to be followed by drinks at the bar and a gala dinner. A very agreeable evening ended with most of our colleagues adjourning to the drawing room for a night cap. By this stage of the evening everyone was very nicely relaxed, and as I entered the drawing room Sir John Hall, of Newcastle, and Ken Bates, from Chelsea, decided to have a lighthearted dig at little old Barnsley's elevation to the top flight. "It's a disgrace – Barnsley

Football Club in the Premier League," Bates yelled across the room, with Sir John chipping in with similar jocular remarks. The pair of them seemed to find it all hugely amusing, but I, having had a glass or two of wine by this point, was determined to stand up for my beloved BFC and my shouted response was something like: "At least you lot have got a proper Football Club now to show you how to do things." A rather unedifying, unchairmanlike but good humoured slanging match then took place across the room, much to the amusement of the rest of the gathering (I hope!). I did, however, promise Bates that one way or another I'd get some revenge when Chelsea came to Barnsley... but more on that later.

After our official induction into the Premier League in June it was back to Oakwell to get on with the hard work of preparing for the Premiership season. On the playing front, very few of the current squad had specific clauses in their contracts outlining improved salaries in the event of promotion to the Premiership, which caused a flood of players wishing to speak to Danny or myself about improved terms. This was understandable and we were sympathetic to their requests, but given the fact that all of them were under contract to the club anyway, we were in a reasonably strong negotiating position. I had earlier made enquiries of chairmen of other smaller top-flight clubs to gain an insight into what kind of wage demands I could expect, and this information proved to be very helpful. Research by experts has shown that the average wage in the Premiership at that time was around £5,000 per week. As we handled contract negotiations with current players, the board also looked to Danny for his recommendations in respect of new signings. The first on his wish list was Slovenian international defender Ales Krizan, who cost the club £269,000 from NK Maribor. Danny had sent a representative to watch Ales play towards the end of the previous season and based on the scout's report, brought him to Oakwell. Sadly, Ales was only a bit-part player at Barnsley, looking short of the necessary quality to play regularly in the Premier League. In fact, quite recently, as part of some consultancy work I do for a produce company, I was offered some Slovenian apples to fulfil one of their contracts. I had a little smile to myself and told the bloke who had offered me the fruit that the last time I had bought something from Slovenia it was a bit of a disaster so I didn't think I'd bother with the apples. Goalkeeper Lars Leese had been on trial at Oakwell during the promotion season and it had been agreed that, if we went up, then we would sign him. Danny wanted a big keeper as back-up to David Watson, and at 6ft 4" Lars, who signed for £274,000, certainly fitted that particular bill. Danny's foreign shopping spree continued with the arrival of South African international midfielder Eric Tinkler, who was playing for Italian outfit Cagliari. Danny and Eric went to see Tinkler in action for his country against England at Old Trafford, and after an impressive performance we bought him for £533,000. Georgi Hristov was the next foreign player on Danny's radar. A Macedonian international who played for Partizan Belgrade, Georgi had earned himself a big reputation in Europe. He was brought to the attention of Danny by the same agent, Alex Kristic, who had introduced us to Marcelle and Bosancic the previous year. Alex and I agreed a deal in principle over the telephone, but it was deemed important that face-to-face negotiations were conducted between Barnsley FC, Partizan Belgrade and the player's agent. Vice-Chairman Barry Taylor and assistant secretary Chris Patzelt were delegated to fly out to Belgrade to complete the deal. Unfortunately, Chris ended up having to travel alone because Barry's passport was stolen in London a few hours before the flight. Chris kept in close touch with me so that I could guide him through the discussions, and following a long day for Chris Patzelt the deal was completed and Georgi went on to sign for Barnsley Football Club for a club record fee of £1.5million. Georgi was clearly a very talented boy, but it could hardly be said that his time in Barnsley was a total success, both on and off the field. Notoriously he was reported to have labelled Barnsley women as 'ugly beer swillers', hardly a statement to endear him to the residents of the town. However, if he'd scored a few more goals, I for one would have forgiven him. The final signing of that summer was Darren Barnard, who arrived at the club a couple of days before the season started from Bristol City for £750,000. We'd come close to

My parents on the beach at Tenby, South Wales.

Me aged seven in my
St Matthew's infant
school uniform.

In the rugby team at Worksop College (fourth from right on back row).

My father, Ernest, in front of the Centre Stand at Oakwell.

The Club's official photo of a young-looking me just after becoming a director.

Danny Wilson, Director Malcolm Hanson and myself, with the construction of the Ora Stand in the background.

In replying to this letter, please write on the envelope:

Number ....   Name ....

NO ANONYMOUS MAIL ALLOWED
NUMBER NAME & WING LETTER
MUST BE ON THE ADDRESS

B

WING B
HMP LINDHOLME
HATFIELD WOODHOUSE
DONCASTER
SOUTH YORKSHIRE
DN7 6EE

Dear Sir
          I Am Writing to you to
Apply As Manager of Barnsley F.C As
Strange As it Might Seem. As you
Can See I Am in Establishment of
one of Her Majestys Prisons, But
Im Being Released Shortly.
          I Have Experience of
Player/Manager in top Amvatee Football
teams Such As Astro who from M/cr
Won the North - west champions of champions
cup who each player plays Semi - Pro.
          I Am A 3rd grade
qualified Coach. I Am in More For
A Violent charge And An Honest Man.
this is not A wind up letter, in
fact if you think Im not Suitable
for this position, Maybe Another position
Might Rise, My Age is 33. look
forward to Hearing from you Soon
                    Good Wishes

No. 243   30141   7/10/63   XMS

One of the more bizarre manager's application that was received.

In the boardroom at Oakwell and in clear need of a haircut.

Much better!

My father and Allan Clarke as he signs his contract.

On the pitch for end of season presentations with Nicky Eaden and Tim Hanfield.

In my work clothes at John Dennis Barnsley Ltd.

Checking into the manager's office.

MARTIN O'NEILL

Dear Sir,   13 Nov '89
            I wish to make formal application for the
post as Manager of Barnsley Football Club. If you are
looking for an "experienced" man who has repeatedly
failed at other Clubs but who is still on the managerial
"merry-go-round" please disregard this letter. However
if you are looking for someone who has fresh
ideas, who can motivate players, deal comfortably
with the media and make the Club successful
again then I promise you I'm the best bet of
all the applications lying on your desk.
            My own playing career, now over through
injury, spanned fourteen years during which time
I played for Nottingham Forest, Manchester City,
Norwich City and Notts County. At Nottingham Forest
I won two European Cup medals, a League
Championship medal, two Littlewood Cup Winners'
     s and many other trophies (Super Cup and

Part of the job application from Martin O'Neill in 1989.

THE WORSHIPFUL THE MAYOR OF BARNSLEY

requests the pleasure of the company of

The Chairman and Lady, Barnsley Football Club

at a reception on the occasion of the visit of
HER MAJESTY QUEEN ELIZABETH II
and
H.R.H. THE PRINCE PHILIP, DUKE OF EDINBURGH
to the METRODOME, BARNSLEY
on Thursday 30th May, 1991 at 10.00am

Invitation to meet the Queen.

My two daughters with the sons of fellow director Ian Potter having just arrived at Wembley.

NATIONWIDE DIVISION ONE PLAY-OFF FINAL

BARNSLEY v IPSWICH TOWN

AT WEMBLEY STADIUM

MONDAY 29th MAY - KICK-OFF 3PM

BARNSLEY

20	Kevin Miller (Gk.)
34	John Curtis
18	Chris Morgan
31	Steve Chettle
28	Keith Brown
11	Darren Barnard
7	Eric Tinkler
8	Craig Hignett (Capt.)
3	Matty Appleby
10	Bruce Dyer
9	Neil Shipperley

Substitutes:

12	Mike Sheron
19	Georgi Hristov
6	Scott Jones
2	Nicky Eaden
16	Geoff Thomas

MANAGER
Dave Bassett

IPSWICH TOWN

1	Richard Wright (Gk.)
25	Gary Croft
3	Jamie Clapham
5	Tony Mowbray
6	Mark Venus
24	John McGreal
8	Matt Holland (Capt.)
11	Jim Magilton
9	David Johnson
27	Marcus Stewart
14	Jermaine Wright

29	Keith Branagan (Gk.)
2	Fabian Wilnis
30	Martijn Reuser
12	Richard Naylor
17	Wayne Brown

MANAGER
George Burley

Referee:	T. Heilbron	(Newton Aycliffe, Co Durham)
Assistant Referees:	D.S. Babski	(Scunthorpe)
	I. Blanchard	(Hull)
Fourth Official:	P. Taylor	(Waltham Cross, Herts)

Team sheet for Wembley.

Barnsley fans outside Wembley.

Ticket for the Royal Box at Wembley.

Nationwide Football League

First Division Play-Off Final - Kick-Off 3.00pm

ADMIT ONE TO

The Royal Box

On Monday 29th May 2000

(via the Banqueting Hall Entrance)

At Wembley.

Myself, my wife and some of my colleagues in the Royal Box at Wembley.

The team and fans at Civic Reception.

Arjan de Zeeuw arriving at the Civic Reception.

Another legend – Toby Tyke.

At a party held in the East Stand to celebrate promotion – with Dr Banarjee, Mick Hayselden and Ian Potter's wife, Dee. It looks like it was a long night!

25 October 2001

FAO Mr John Dennis
Chairman
Barnsley Football Club Ltd
Oakwell Ground
Grove Street
BARNSLEY

Dear Mr Dennis,

REF: VACANT MANAGERS JOB(1ST TEAM ONLY)

Myself and my friend are writing with regards to you considering
us for the vacant post at Barnsley Football Club of 1st team
manager and assistant.

My friend, who originates from Elsecar, Barnsley informs me that
you are a fruit and veg magnate who is down to earth and would
listen to our application!

My track record is as manager of a local football team called
Flixton FC, who play in the Scarborough and district third
division and finished third last season just outside a promotion
place. We trained hard throughout the week in most of the
Scarborough pubs but still could not find that extra needed for
success.

Our finest moment came when we reached the final of the local
Junior Country Cup. However, we got stuffed 3-0 on the night
against a very big team, who all looked like lard-arses! The lads
were down for about an hour until the stripper began her routine!

If you consider myself and my good friend as number two, i'm sure
we will be the apple of the fans eyes, whilst sending them
bananas with our style of play. It would be a plum job for us,
however if things went pear shaped we would not have any sour
grapes for being released from our post.

We already have a centre forward lined up who peppers the onion
bag on a regular basis, whilst we also have a top defender who
will plug the leaks at the back! We would apease the fans with
our style of off the ball running bean a strength of our play.
We also have a player who can nick the ball of an opposing
players feet and if I was playing, play it tomatoes.If any
players were to step out of line my number two would be able
turnip it in the bud before things got out of hand.

If you could orange an interview we would be grapefull, where we

One of the many quirky job applications I received.

Danny and myself at a Player of the Year Dinner. Judging from the intensity of the discussion, it looks like Danny was talking about a new contract!

With Malcolm Hanson, then chief of ORA at a Player of the Year Dinner.

With my wife, Christianne on a cruise.

landing Darren earlier in the summer, were unable to agree terms with his club but went back with an improved offer to get our man. Darren was a very talented attack-minded left-back with a cultured left foot, and he became a very popular player during his time at Barnsley.

The board had given Danny the support that he'd asked for in the transfer market, but we had prudently held some funds back should further team strengthening be necessary during the season. In hindsight we made a mistake by not recruiting players with Premier League pedigree. Although Thompson, Wilkinson and Hendrie had some experience of the top flight, they were unlikely to play a full part in the Premier League season. As a comparison Southampton, having had a difficult start to the season, signed David Hirst, Carlton Palmer and Kevin Richardson. Those three were thirty-somethings who were battle-hardened, experienced Premier League players whose contribution to Southampton's relegation battle was enormous. The contrast between those three and the type of player that we had signed was very stark. Nonetheless, we weren't in the Premier League just to make the numbers up, and with the sense that it was going to be us against the world for a whole season, we genuinely believed in our survival chances, particularly with Danny Wilson at the helm.

The whole summer flashed by in a blur of activity with barely a day passing without a meeting of some description. There was unprecedented interest in Barnsley Football Club both from the local and national media and I found myself being canvassed to provide interviews on a regular basis. I was always at pains to point out to whoever came to see me that I did not want our Football Club and our town to be portrayed in the stereotypical 'flat cap and whippet' manner that had been the case for so many years. The Football Club had created history for itself and the town by gaining promotion and although we were intending to enjoy ourselves, it was our intention to be competitive. During that summer I found the press to be, by and large, helpful and supportive although when I first became chairman, I had been advised by a former director to treat the press with great caution. I took the view that I needed to establish good relationships with as many members of the press corps as I could because that was in the best interests of Barnsley Football Club. There were some occasions when I would take a member of the press into my confidence but ask him to spin a particular story in a certain way, and only once did I ever get let down. I was recently reminded of that particular incident by the current Chairman of Tranmere Rovers, Peter Johnson, who apparently had witnessed me pinning some unfortunate press guy against the wall before threatening to have him ejected from the stadium – he had let me down rather badly. Over the years, though, I was fortunate enough to have had good relationships with the vast majority of the press. I shall always have a soft spot for Barry Foster, formerly of the *Yorkshire Post*, and Janine Self, formerly of *The Sun* but now of the *Daily Mail*, who were very kind and helpful to me in my early days as chairman. A group of journalists based in the north comprising of Ian Appleyard, of the *Yorkshire Post*, Mike Morgan, from *The Sun*, John Edwards, of the *Express*, Alan Biggs, who was a freelance journalist, and Peter Ferguson, of the *Daily Mail*, formed the core of my press contacts, and on a local level I made it my business to be as honest and open as possible with journalists from the *Sheffield Star* and, of course, our own *Barnsley Chronicle*. The club's relationship with the *Chronicle* could sometimes be difficult but, as the chairman of the board I totally accepted that it was their job to reflect the views of their readers. It was my belief that the *Chronicle* needed the club as much as the club needed the *Chronicle* but I appreciated that the paper was not an arm of the Football Club's publicity machine. Former Sports Editor Keith Lodge and I enjoyed a very cordial working relationship over the years, although I realised that that relationship would not spare me or the club from possible criticism. Nonetheless, an incident occurred just before Easter in 1995 when the *Chronicle* overstepped the mark, allowing a letter to appear in the sports pages outrageously claiming that the directors of the club were lining their own pockets. After consultation with my colleagues I was authorised to instruct lawyers and within hours counsel's opinion advised us that we had a strong case against the paper. After meetings with the owners and the editor, it was agreed that subject to them meeting the costs of our lawyers and a full apology being published the following week, the matter could be laid to rest.

The Premiership season was now upon us and our first eagerly awaited top flight challenge came in the shape of West Ham United at Oakwell on 9 August. Optimism abounded around the club and the town and a packed crowd went wild when Neil Redfearn gave us the lead with an early header. It seemed we were on our way to our first three points, but despite dominating the match we finished on the wrong end of a 2-1 scoreline, and that was the first harsh lesson of what life was going to be like at the highest level. So often during that Premiership season we would suffer defeat but then bounce back with a good win, and that's exactly what happened a few days after the West Ham game when we opened our points tally with a great away win at Crystal Palace. That put us in confident mood for our first ever live Premiership television appearance when Chelsea were due to visit Oakwell the following Sunday. The Chelsea party was staying at Whitley Hall Hotel, near Sheffield, the night before the game. Chairman Ken Bates had rather irritatingly enquired of Barry Taylor if there were any restaurants good enough for him to eat at in the north of England. Barry and I, along with our wives, decided we would invite Mr Bates, his partner Susannah Constantine, and Chelsea Chief Executive Colin Hutchinson, to join us for dinner at the excellent Armstrongs Restaurant on Dodworth Road, Barnsley. I arranged for a member of my staff, who occasionally drove me to specific evening functions, to provide the transport. He collected the Chelsea delegates from Whitley Hall, but I had instructed him to drive past Armstrongs and stop at the fish and chip shop at the bottom of Dodworth Road. This he did and Ken, Susannah and Colin got out. My driver told them that they would find the Dennises and Taylors at a table at the back of the chip shop. They quickly realised that they were the victim of a practical joke from the Barnsley chairman and when they finally arrived at Armstrongs I was subjected to yet more good humoured abuse from Mr Bates – but it was worth it just to get my revenge. The following day we entertained Chelsea at Oakwell and got hammered 6-0. We were totally outplayed with the likes of

Leboeuf, Zola and Vialli being simply too good for us. This was the first of a number of hidings that we took during the Premier League season, and although our fans remained in high spirits, it was certainly no laughing matter for this chairman.

Following the Chelsea humiliation the team bounced back to beat Bolton 2-1 in the midweek, but Danny was starting to realise that he needed to bolster the strike force. Paul Wilkinson was finding it difficult to make an impact on his return to the top flight and was soon to depart to Millwall for a fee of £150,000. Danny expressed a wish to bring in West Ham striker Iain Dowie, a big, burly front man who had fallen out of favour at Upton Park. Danny knew Dowie from his Northern Ireland days, so it was arranged that we'd meet the player and his representative – ex-Barnsley midfielder Mick McGuire – at the Ardsley House Hotel. We knew that Dowie, who was likely to cost around £1million, was on decent money at West Ham, but because he wasn't getting regular football we were confident of landing him. Dowie's demands were higher than we had expected and although I found myself making a more generous offer than I had originally intended, Dowie and his agent were still not satisfied. They disappeared to another room to talk the matter over and in their absence I told Danny that I thought we'd gone too far and I hoped they'd turn the offer down, which thankfully they did. However, we left it with them that if they had a change of mind then they should get back to us within the next couple of days – we never heard from them again and I for one thought we had a lucky escape. Danny then turned his attention to Ashley Ward of Derby Country, who were our opponents at Pride Park that weekend. This gave me the opportunity to speak directly to my counterpart at Derby, Lionel Pickering. He demanded £1.5million, which I thought was too much and eventually got him to compromise on a guaranteed fee of £1.31million, with a sell-on clause that gave Derby twenty per cent of any profit that we might make should the player be sold. My logic in suggesting this was that Ward had never gone anywhere for more than £500,000 before this deal and in view of the fact that we were paying two and a half times that figure, I thought it unlikely that he would move on for much more than that in the future – another great decision by the Barnsley chairman. Having agreed the fee with Derby we agreed terms with the player, and Ashley Ward became the most highly rewarded player in the history of Barnsley Football Club with a contract worth around £5,000 per week.

Despite Ward's addition and the impressive start to his Barnsley career, results did not improve. Having lost at Derby we were thumped at Everton 4-2 before a bad defeat at Wimbledon 4-1, and another poor day followed with a 2-0 home defeat to Leicester City. However, if ever there was a match when you realised how hard the Premier League was it would have to be the 5-0 battering we received at Highbury against Arsenal. I had joined the team as they travelled to their hotel at Waltham Abbey, just off the M25, in readiness for the match the following day. At dinner with Danny and Eric Winstanley I had asked them what their tactics were going to be the following day. They explained in some detail what the plan was, with Eric Tinkler playing a key role as a spare man in front of the back four to pick up the threat of the likes of Dennis Bergkamp. The next day I had the privilege of a luxury limousine ride to Highbury to do a *Football Focus* interview before settling down in my seat in the directors' box for the real business of the day. For the first twenty-five minutes the plan worked perfectly, and we even came close to taking the lead through an Arjan de Zeeuw header, brilliantly saved by David Seaman. However, a few minutes later Dennis Bergkamp picked the ball up in the inside left position, Tinkler was a split second late in closing him down and two touches later, the ball was flying passed David Watson's outstretched left arm and into the corner of the net – 1-0 to Arsenal. By half-time we were 3-0 down and it was hard to work out what had happened – we had gone from being on level terms to being on the receiving end of a thrashing – all within fifteen minutes. We went on to lose 5-0 to Arsenal and were shown the class and quality that was to see them lift the double that season. Off the field the Gunners were equally impressive, their hospitality being the finest that we received on our Premier League travels.

We picked things up with a win against Coventry, Ward getting his first goal in Barnsley colours, which left us with a visit to Old Trafford to look forward to the following weekend. Arriving in Manchester buoyed by the previous week's result, our hopes were destroyed when we were hammered 7-0 and, to coin a well-used football phrase, we were lucky to get nil. On a personal note I had my family with me and Christianne's entrance to Old Trafford was spectacular. Unfortunately as she approached the reception area her heel caught in a grate and she made a very impressive entrance into the Theatre of Dreams headfirst landing on her knees. I guess that just about summed up our day. My daughters sat behind us during the game and I could hear frequent whispers and giggles coming from them throughout the match. I was trying to focus on what was happening on the pitch, but they were clearly more interested in the fact that Posh Spice was sat behind them. I have to admit that I didn't know who 'Posh Spice' was, or even who the Spice Girls were come to that, although if they had played in our back four that day we might have done better.

Following another pasting, this time at Southampton, Danny went out and signed big Swedish centre-half Peter Markstedt for £200,000. He went straight into the team for the match at Anfield against the mighty Liverpool and both he and Lars Leese, who had been preferred in goal to David Watson, performed heroics in our 1-0 win. We got battered from start to finish, but a goal from Ward, who was also immense on that memorable day, somehow gave us a barely-credible and thoroughly flukey three points. In this rollercoaster season of high hopes and shattered dreams our faith was once more restored, although an undeserved 3-2 home defeat against Leeds United at Oakwell, after we had taken a two-goal lead, once more put us in the doldrums. Eight days after that we had the much anticipated clash with our friends from Sheffield at Hillsborough, which was due to be the live Sky Monday night game. We acquitted ourselves well that night and looked to be heading for a 1-1 draw and a well-deserved point before Paulo Di Canio who, it could be argued should have been sent off earlier in the match, stole a late winner. We picked up useful points against Newcastle at Oakwell and in the Boxing Day clash at Bolton, but suffered another humiliating defeat early in the New Year against West Ham where we went down 6-0 with a young Chris Morgan making his debut for Barnsley.

Our attention then turned to the FA Cup and after beating Premiership rivals Bolton 1-0 at Oakwell in the third round, we earned a battling 1-1 draw with Tottenham at White Hart Lane. We welcomed Spurs back to Oakwell for the replay – a game that was won comfortably 3-1 with goals from Ward, Redfearn and Barnard. The win earned us a fifth round trip to Old Trafford to face the might of Manchester United once more. Memories of October's debacle were still quite raw, as were Christianne's knees, but the cup tie saw us give a much better account of ourselves. John Hendrie scored the opener after a mistake by United keeper Peter Schmeichel, who had sliced a clearance in John's direction. He pounced on it as fast as his little legs would carry him to beat the Danish keeper to the ball and slide it into the net. Unsurprisingly the Barnsley contingent, including those in the directors' box, went wild, but our spirits were dampened by Sheringham's equaliser just before half-time. Nonetheless, we did enough to earn a 1-1 draw, although in the last few minutes we had an absolute dead cert penalty appeal turned down for a trip on Andy Liddell by Gary Neville. Referee Mike Riley waved play on, which meant that Ferguson's United were to travel to Barnsley for the cup replay at Oakwell the following week. The upside to Riley's bad decision meant that at least we would be able to cash in on a big gate at Oakwell for the replay. Of all the matches that season to my mind the replay will go down as the most memorable, as we beat United on our own turf 3-2. John Hendrie hit the first from the left-hand edge of the penalty box with the outside of his right foot, although he looked half a yard offside when the ball was played through. Our second came on the stroke of half-time with a thumping header from young centre-half Scott Jones. Teddy Sheringham, who had started the game on the bench, pulled one back for United ten minutes after the break, but Scott Jones again headed home to complete an unlikely brace. With ten minutes left Andy Cole narrowed the margin to create an unbelievably tense finale to the match. Happily we held out for a famous victory.

By that stage of the season it's fair to say that all of the fans, and even some of us within the Football Club, had started to buy into the conspiracy theory that all referees were against us because nobody really wanted Barnsley in the Premier League. Early in the replay a number of refereeing decisions had gone against us and the vice-chairman and I were being quite vocal in our views. United's manager, who was sat close to us in the visiting directors' box, made it clear that he wasn't very impressed by the undignified behaviour of the Barnsley officials. After the game, as I was on my way to congratulate Danny and his staff, I bumped into Mr Ferguson as he too was heading into the manager's office for his customary glass of red wine. I thought it appropriate to offer my commiserations to him and to wish him all the best for the big European Cup tie the following week, but before I could open my mouth, in typical Fergie fashion, with his familiar Glaswegian accent, he snorted: "You'll not be complaining about the referee now, will you, Mr Chairman?" I was fortunate enough to meet Sir Alex on a number of social occasions after that night and he always appeared interested in how things were going at Barnsley. That great victory against United in the replay earned us a sixth round tie at St James's Park to face Newcastle United. The tie took place on a Sunday afternoon in early March but ended in a disappointing 3-1 defeat with Adie Moses being sent off. That decision was a complete travesty because Adie had been the subject of persistent fouling by Alan Shearer all afternoon but never got a decision. After the game, when I was asked for my comments, I queried whether Shearer was being sponsored by the World Wildlife Fund in view of the protection he was getting. But at least we could now concentrate on the league.

Our league form remained patchy and although Ashley Ward was proving to be an inspired signing the team was still short of goals so Danny turned his attention to financially-troubled Sheffield United who, it was rumoured, were prepared to offload Norwegian striker Jan Aage Fjortoft. I spoke to the chief executive at Bramall Lane, Charles Green who, coincidentally, had played a few games for Barnsley Reserves in the 1970s. We agreed a deal to bring Fjortoft to Oakwell for £800,000 and it struck me as odd that the Blades were reportedly on the brink of selling Brian Deane to Leeds United at the same time. The news that they were prepared to sell their two star strikers angered many of the Bramall Lane faithful, to the point where the traditional Saturday evening car park protest was actually brought forward by forty-eight hours! On a serious note I had a feeling that they might pull out of the deal so Danny and I arranged for Jan Aage to be at Oakwell at 9am the following morning to discuss his personal terms. Jan was a bright, intelligent, articulate man who handled his own negotiations with some aplomb. Agreement was reached for Jan to became a Barnsley player. In his fifteen appearances for Barnsley in the Premier League season Jan scored six goals, two of which came in a 2-1 home triumph against Wimbledon at the end of February, whilst Ashley Ward chipped in with eight from twenty-nine appearances, one of which was the winner in a 1-0 away victory at Villa Park the week after the win over the Crazy Gang. A 4-3 home win over Southampton on 14 March meant for the first and only time in our Premiership lives we had won three matches on the trot, and following a weekend break for internationals we looked forward to our home clash with Liverpool with a spring in our step and renewed belief that we could confound the critics.

If ever there was to be a seminal moment in our season then that game against Liverpool on 28 March was it. History records that the score was Barnsley 2 Liverpool 3 with Redfearn netting twice for Barnsley and the visitors' goals coming from Riedle (two) and McManaman. But those brief statistics in no way reflect the events of that emotionally charged afternoon. The central figure of the match was, sadly, the referee, Mr Gary Willard from Worthing. Mr Willard was an Inland Revenue officer in civilian life and it's a shame that he didn't concentrate on his full-time career because that day he lost control of a football match in a manner that I have never come across before or since. He sent off three Barnsley players – Darren Barnard, Chris Morgan and Darren Sheridan – as well as apparently abandoning play, leaving the pitch without consulting the managers, the players or the police. His erratic behaviour was the cause of a minor pitch invasion by a tiny number of Barnsley fans who had simply overreacted to the events as conducted by Mr Willard. Thankfully, quick thinking and even quicker action by our own Jan Aage Fjortoft and Liverpool's Paul Ince prevented the interlopers from reaching the referee, who eventually came to his senses and re-started the match. The final insult on a crazy afternoon was when Steve McManaman got Liverpool's winner in injury time. From a personal point of view it was crucial that I kept as clear a head as possible as I faced arguably the most testing hour in my time as chairman of Barnsley Football Club. I was under siege from all sections of the media with microphones and cameras being pushed in my face at every end and turn. I like to think that I managed to act in a dignified and restrained manner, but I also hope that I managed to get across my frustration in respect of the referee's performance. Even at that stage we at Barnsley knew that there would be an FA inquiry into the events of that afternoon, but fortunately the inquiry was not held until after the season's end, and we were lucky to escape with a small fine and a warning as to our future conduct. One of the great traditions at Barnsley Football Club, at that time and for many years previously, was that the chairman would automatically go in to see the referee after the game to offer him a drink. He would then nip off to the bar and return to hand out the drinks and have a chat with the officials. It was a great way of bridging the gap between the club and the referees and gave both parties the opportunity to have an informal chat and get to know each other. This tradition had always been greatly appreciated by referees and contributed to our well-earned reputation for being warm and hospitable hosts. I have to say, though, that there was only one occasion during my tenure as chairman when I did not follow this particular tradition, and I don't think anyone would be surprised to know it was on that fatal day after the Liverpool match. I had no desire to exchange pleasantries with Mr Willard that evening, nor was I sure that I would have been able to retain my dignity. Looking back, on the afternoon of 28 March 1998, it is my belief that Barnsley Football Club was relegated from the Premiership, not mathematically of course but because of the fallout from that day. We were to lose three key players to suspension and the emotion and drama of the Liverpool game meant that a Football Club that was coming close to running on empty needed to find reserves of energy and passion that had already been used up.

We barely had time to draw breath before Tuesday night saw us in action once again, away at Blackburn Rovers. A Georgi Hristov equaliser looked to have earned us a vital point until once more the fates conspired against us as substitute Kevin Gallacher notched a late winner for the home team. As we trooped dejectedly away from Ewood Park that night, we knew we had to gird our loins yet again for another massive encounter away at Elland Road the following Saturday. Once more, a Hristov strike a minute before half-time looked to have set us on our way to a crucial draw, but an unfortunate own goal by Reds' defender Adie Moses ten minutes from time again saw us leave empty handed. To compound our miserable afternoon, record signing Hristov was given his marching orders for verbally abusing a linesman – the second time that season that Georgi's broken English had managed to get him into trouble. After a traumatic week in the life of Barnsley Football Club we had played three matches, getting no points and we'd had four players sent off. Remarkably, we found the strength and reserves to beat Sheffield Wednesday 2-1 at Oakwell the following Saturday, but after a disappointing defeat at Newcastle United we could only manage a 1-1 draw against relegation rivals Tottenham, who had struggled all season under Swiss manager Christian Gross, when really only a win would have been good enough. There were three games left, the first of which was at home to champions elect Arsenal, the final match of our Premiership season was to be against eventual runners-up Manchester United, with a visit to Leicester City sandwiched in between. Arsenal achieved a comfortable 2-0 victory at Oakwell, which meant that only a win at Filbert Street could keep our faint hopes alive. We travelled to Leicester with high hopes, but a very subdued Barnsley performance resulted in a bitterly disappointing 1-0 defeat. That, and other results that day, confirmed our relegation back to Division One and the dream was over. It was a very sad and emotional day for all connected with Barnsley Football Club and tears were shed by players, supporters and, dare I say it, directors as well. After the game I crossed the pitch to applaud the travelling Barnsley contingent for their commitment to the club throughout that season and to let them know that we at the club felt as desolate as they did. I was desperately keen to have a chat with Danny as soon as possible and after we had both done brief interviews with *Match of the Day* and he had finished his round of other media interviews, I finally managed to buttonhole him and we found a quiet moment away from the maelstrom in the away team's dugout at Filbert Street. There had been a continuing whirl of speculation about Danny's intentions should the club be relegated, so I asked him point blank what he wanted to do. I was rather taken aback when he asked me if I was going to sack him – a thought that had never entered my head. I told him not to be so stupid and to give me a proper answer. I think he was pleased to know that we all still held him in such high regard and after our brief chat we both agreed that when the dust had settled on the season, we'd find a way to have another go.

The curtain came down on that historic season on 10 May 1998, as Manchester United cantered to a comfortable 2-0 win at Oakwell. Our supporters had been in high spirits all season and on that emotive day they didn't disappoint. It remains a huge regret of mine that we failed in our target that season, but looking back, without emotion, we quite simply weren't good enough. Our thirty-five-point tally was not embarrassingly low, and since that season teams have stayed up with fewer points, but for us, it was not meant to be. Our goal tally of thirty-seven was as much of a problem as the eighty-two that we conceded, but Barnsley Football Club won many friends that season, both for itself and for the town. In reviewing my hundreds of files from my time as chairman, I came across some interesting facts and figures from our Premier League season. The club's turnover had grown to £12million – it was just £1.6million in my first year as chairman; we received £5.4million in television and commercial revenue from the Premier League – a mere drop in the ocean compared to the current era; the overall wage bill at the club was just over £4million (it was £862,000 when I was first chairman); and unbelievably, the club shop had sales of over £1million compared to the £14,777 that it was in 1990. We became known as everyone's second favourite team, but that was little consolation as the harsh realities of life in the Premiership supported my theory, that there are very few fairytales in football and ours was not to be one of them.

CHAPTER 10

Back to Reality

Following relegation the directors met to review the events of the season and to consolidate our plans for the next season and beyond. One of the pressing issues that we had expected to deal with was the future of the manager, but following my chat with Danny after the Leicester game I was able to report to the board that Danny had indicated that he wanted to stay and try and do it all over again. Whilst I was pleased that he had said this, I still felt slightly uneasy. Towards the end of the promotion season Danny had agreed a new three-year deal, which involved substantially improved terms. The contract included a clause specifying the salary he would be due to for any period that the club spent in the Premier League, but which also stipulated that following relegation he would revert to his salary as a First Division manager. After discussion with the board, it was agreed that Danny should continue to receive his Premiership salary for one further year as a gesture of appreciation from the directors. I told Danny of the board's decision and off he went on holiday in great spirits. He'd previously not expressed a great desire to change the squad in any meaningful way, believing that the players at his disposal would be good enough to mount another promotion challenge. That always presumed that the speculation surrounding Ashley Ward, after his massive performances in the Premier League, and renewed rumours about the future of Neil Redfearn, would come to nothing.

The likelihood of Neil staying at Barnsley had already started to recede, particularly due to the fact that earlier in the year he had signed up with well-known football agent Mel Stein, who at the time also represented Paul Gascoigne. Mel was a qualified lawyer who came with a formidable reputation, and who in the February had contacted me to announce that he was representing Neil Redfearn and wanted to negotiate a better contract for his new client. I responded by suggesting that we wait until the end of the season because we were in the middle of a relegation battle and I wanted our captain and inspiration to be focused on the job in hand. Mel was insistent that talks should take place immediately and faxed me through some rather interesting proposals. The specific wage demands were high, but there were other clauses that caught my attention suggesting, for instance, that Neil would always have to be guaranteed to be the highest paid player at the Football Club. My view of these proposals was that it was an agent getting busy to try and impress his new client rather than the fact that Neil genuinely believed that what was being put forward was reasonable. I must stress that the situation in no way affected Neil's contribution on the pitch nor his relationship with either myself or Danny. Having batted away Mr Stein until the end of the season, I agreed to meet him at his offices off Park Lane in London in early May, but was disappointed to find that Neil and his wife were there because as I explained earlier, my preference was always to talk business with the agent without the player being present. The meeting commenced with Mr Stein informing me that there was strong interest in Neil from other clubs, indicating that he could orchestrate a transfer for his client away from Barnsley. It became clear that both parties remained a long way apart and I left London that day resigned to the fact that we would be losing our captain. Neil eventually went to newly promoted Charlton Athletic for an initial £850,000 plus appearance money, which took the deal up to £1million. It was a sad day when Neil Redfearn left Barnsley Football Club and I remain convinced that without the intervention of Mr Stein it probably wouldn't have happened. Neil never really produced the kind of form that he'd enjoyed at Barnsley again in his career, but there were no recriminations from either party when he left. He and I remain on good terms to this very day.

Continued speculation rumbled on about the future of our manager, which was having an unsettling effect amongst the supporters. Particularly alarming was the reported interest from Sheffield Wednesday where, of course, Danny had been a popular player. Wednesday had been linked with a number of high profile managers to fill their vacant post, but when it was announced that they were on the brink of appointing Scottish manager Walter Smith, the board and I were able to breathe a sigh of relief. However, at the eleventh hour those discussions collapsed, Wednesday were back to square one and I feared the worst. It was the summer of the World Cup in France and prior to myself and friends making the journey to Paris for the final I was obviously watching England's progress on television. The fateful phone call came during half-time of extra time in the nail-biting contest between England and Argentina. I answered, to be greeted with the following words from the Chairman of Sheffield Wednesday, Dave Richards: "I'm so sorry John; this is the call that I never wanted to make, but can we please have permission to speak to your manager, Danny Wilson?" I responded by very succinctly suggesting that he leave me alone and that we'd talk the next day. I was deeply troubled by the phone call and was aware that the pull of Sheffield Wednesday would probably be too great for Danny to resist. I was also greatly concerned that so late in the close season, with the players due to report back for training the following Monday, we were likely to be losing the best manager in the history of Barnsley Football Club. After that phone call I tried to watch the last few minutes of the England match, which turned out to be as depressing as the phone call, and I went to bed expecting not to sleep much. That turned out to be the case as I turned things over in my mind all night. Critics will say that if we didn't want Danny to leave then we shouldn't have informed him of Sheffield Wednesday's interest, but he and I had a gentleman's agreement whereby I would always inform him if enquiries were received from other clubs. In return he would let me know if unofficial approaches were made to him. On previous occasions West Bromwich Albion and Luton Town, for whom Danny had played a major part in winning the League Cup earlier in his career, had approached me for permission to talk to Danny and on both occasions he asked me to pass on his thanks for their interest but that he had a job to do at Barnsley. Nonetheless, I had a strong feeling that this time it would be different and the following day, after consulting with my Vice-Chairman Barry Taylor and the rest of the board, I arranged to meet Danny at Oakwell to inform him of the approach from Sheffield Wednesday. As I expected, he did nothing to make me think that he would stay at Barnsley but said that he needed to talk to his wife and family before speaking to me again. I clarified with Danny the fact that, until compensation had been agreed, he would not have the club's permission to speak to Sheffield Wednesday, and at that stage he assured me that they had not approached him directly. His contract contained our by now traditional one-year pay-off clause whereby we would be due a full year's salary if a manager left us for another club. I explained to Danny that it was my intention to try and do a little bit better than his contract allowed and asked him, as one last gesture to Barnsley Football Club, not to discuss his contract details until we had reached agreement with our 'friends' from Hillsborough. I then spoke to Mr Richards demanding £2million in compensation and he, unsurprisingly, wouldn't agree such a sum but said he'd get back to me. In the subsequent conversation he explained that, in view of our hugely optimistic demands, there was little point in wasting time trying to negotiate so they were intending to proceed to talk to Danny with or without our permission as they were perfectly happy for the dispute to be settled by arbitration. This was clearly not in Barnsley's interest because the compensation figure was perfectly clear in Danny's contract, so I had some back peddling to do. Finally, after much toing and froing, some heated debate and eventually some common sense discussion, a compensation figure was agreed at £500,000 – approximately double that which we were due under the terms of the contract. Whilst it was pleasing to have made the most of a difficult situation, there was no satisfaction in seeing Danny leave Oakwell. Ultimately, Barnsley Football Club found itself in a familiar position where a so-called 'big club' had blown us out of the water financially. During my talks with Danny I made it clear to him that we would move heaven and earth to try and keep him at the club, and to be fair to him he revealed that earlier that summer he had been approached by Everton, but it was the lure of Sheffield Wednesday that was the decisive factor. The rumour mill around Barnsley claimed that Wilson's move to Wednesday had been agreed weeks previously, and that the announcement was delayed until we had sold our season tickets. This was absolutely not the case and we, the board, were as devastated as the fans at the loss of Danny Wilson. People branded him Judas and he went from hero to villain in the space of twenty-four hours. Danny was an ambitious man who was taking what he thought was a step up the managerial ladder. I would suggest to any fan at any football club that if they were offered double or treble wages to work for a competitor in the same industry, they would not refuse, and that's precisely the situation Danny Wilson found himself in during the summer of 1998. The board and I were devastated to see Danny leave the club but understood the dilemma he faced. We never felt any sense of betrayal, just enormous gratitude for the success that he had helped bring to the Football Club.

As part and parcel of running a football club you regularly muse on any potential managerial targets in the event of you finding yourself looking for a new manager. Because of Danny's success, this was a process that regularly exercised my mind and the board and I had talked generally about what we might do should Danny depart. John Hendrie, who had been inspirational during the promotion season, was a vastly experienced player with a strong and lively character and a good knowledge of the game as well as being one of the leaders in the dressing room. We felt that if the job became vacant, John would make a good choice, although because of his lack of experience he'd clearly need the support of a strong backroom staff. Given the timing of Danny's departure – there were only two days between him leaving and the players reporting back for training – we believed that we needed to act swiftly to end any uncertainty at the club, so it was agreed that I would contact John Hendrie to discuss the possibility of him becoming the next Barnsley manager. A weekend of intense discussion took place with it ending in us reaching agreement with John for him to become manager with Peter Shirtliff becoming assistant manager, and the trusty Eric Winstanley retaining his position as first team coach. Eric was on the road to recovery from heart surgery but it was envisaged that he would be well enough to play an important part in the new regime. Discussions had taken place long into the night on the Sunday evening at the Bramhope Post House close to John's home, and on the Monday morning a meeting was arranged with the players to introduce them to their new boss. The response from the squad was both surprised but supportive as John had been a popular member of the dressing room and was a respected senior pro. John knew that he had a big task ahead of him, not the least of which was to try and fill the boots of the now departed Redfearn. He wanted to bring in proven quality and the signings of Robin van der Laan, from Derby County, for £325,000, and the vastly experienced Kevin Richardson, from Southampton for £30,000, having enjoyed a terrific career with Everton, Arsenal and Aston Villa, bolstered the midfield. The season began with a 2-2 draw against West Bromwich Albion before we suffered a rather alarming 3-1 defeat at Crewe Alexandra. At the time Crewe boasted the likes of Dean Ashton and Rob Hulse in their ranks and were a decent side, but we were really poor that day and our woes were increased when George Hristov suffered a knee injury that ruled him out for most of the season.

Following the receipt of our parachute payment and the transfer fee received for Neil Redfearn, bolstered by a further £350,000 from Wigan for Andy Liddell, we were in a position to support John financially as he looked to strengthen the squad. John expressed an interest in signing Bruce Dyer from Crystal Palace. They were a club in financial turmoil so it was felt that there was the possibility of a bargain. An approach was made to the Selhurst Park club officials about the availability of Bruce, who some years earlier had become the first £1million teenager in British football. Bruce would confess to having had a wayward lifestyle in his early years in football, but had turned his life round completely and become a committed

Christian. His father, George, who shared the same strong religious beliefs as his son, acted as Bruce's agent, but they managed to put their Christian charity to one side when negotiating a very good contract for Bruce. In all fairness to them, although our discussions were tortuous Bruce took a pay cut to leave Palace because he was keen to start a new life in the north of England, and signed for a fee of £680,000. Bruce became a popular player at Oakwell, scoring more than sixty goals in 180 games and having settled in the South Yorkshire countryside remains as charming and as likeable as he always was. I've bumped into him a number of times over recent years – and slightly embarrassingly, he always calls me 'Mr Chairman', as so many of our former players do.

John's next major signing was Craig Hignett, who at the time was playing football with Aberdeen. John knew Craig from their time together at Middlesbrough and Hignett, like John, had found himself out in the cold when 'Boro embarked on their policy of signing big name foreign players. Craig had found it difficult to settle in Scotland and it was reported that he would be interested in moving back south of the border. I spoke to his agent Struan Marshall, who gave me some idea of the kind of contract that Hignett had at Aberdeen. Because he had signed on a Bosman free transfer, Aberdeen had invested what would have been a sizeable transfer fee into his contract, which had two and a half years to run. This meant that negotiations would be difficult, but having agreed a fee with Aberdeen of £800,000 for the player, we then overcame any issues regarding his personal terms by increasing the fee by £100,000, which Aberdeen were able to pass on to Hignett in respect of the termination of his contract. Marshall also represented our player Martin Bullock, and in actual fact the original deal would have seen Martin going to Aberdeen as part of the package with Martin being valued at £400,000. But having visited the granite city on a particularly inhospitable Scottish day, Martin chose to remain at Oakwell and fight for his place. Hignett signed on the Thursday morning and went straight into the team for our Friday night live TV game against Huddersfield Town. That match will stay in the memories of Barnsley fans – and probably a few Huddersfield ones as well – for many a year, as we trounced our West Yorkshire visitors 7-1, having led 6-0 at half-time. Hignett marked his debut by scoring twice and only missed out on a hat-trick because he blazed a second-half penalty over the bar. Bruce Dyer also hit the net twice that night, but the highlight of the evening was a fantastic goal scored by Darren Barnard – a strike that I believe is the best I've ever seen at Oakwell. Nicky Eaden crossed the ball from the right flank to the left hand edge of the penalty area where Darren ran in and smashed a volley into the top right hand corner. The irony behind Barnard's wonder strike was that he had very nearly left the club that same week. A deal had been agreed for Darren to go to Southampton and in return, we were to sign the experienced Carlton Palmer as well as receiving a generous cash settlement. Darren and his agent, Ian Elliott, spent two days in contract talks with Southampton but, in spite of the fact that he was offered terms that would have almost doubled his money, surprisingly he decided to continue his career at Barnsley. News of the proposed deal had leaked out and given the fact that Barnard was popular at Oakwell and that Carlton Palmer, due to his previous affiliation with a club who play in blue and white stripes, wasn't so popular, I knew I was in for some stick that night. When Darren's strike hit the back of the net the chants of 'There's Only One Darren Barnard' rang around Oakwell and I shuffled rather uncomfortably in my seat, knowing how close we had come to selling the player. An interesting thought about that night against Huddersfield Town is that it was the only occasion that Hignett, Dyer and Ward all lined up in a league game together. Who knows what might have happened if we'd been in a position to pick all three in the same team for the rest of the season.

A major problem that John Hendrie had to deal with during the early months of his career as a manager was the constant, almost daily speculation about the future of Ashley Ward. His performances for the club, both during the Premiership and in the early part of the 1998-99 season, had made Ward one of the most sought after strikers around, with the greatest interest coming from Leeds United, under David O'Leary, and Leicester City, managed by Martin O'Neill. Leeds were the first to make a move, offering a straight £2million, but in my conversation with Mr O'Leary, it became clear that that was their first and final offer. As twenty per cent of any profit on the fee paid for Ward was owed to his previous club, Derby County, the board rejected O'Leary's offer, genuinely believing that we would do better. Having had a number of conversations with O'Neill, his interest manifested itself in a rather more dramatic way when I attended a meeting of all Pontins League clubs at Hillsborough. I bumped into Martin as he came out of the lift and he dramatically dropped to his knees and held his hands out in supplication begging me to sell him Ashley Ward. He already knew that we'd turned down £2million and was trying to persuade his directors to up the ante. Ward's agent, Colin Gordon, was in regular contact with me telling me that we needed to sell as Wardy could earn a lot more money elsewhere, with my response being that we would sell when we were good and ready and that he and his client would have to trust me. I always felt confident that we could do better than the £2million price tag that the media appeared to have put on Ward's head, but we didn't seem to get away from that figure until fortune turned in our favour when it was reported that Blackburn Rovers had agreed terms with Dion Dublin, of Coventry City, for a fee in excess of £4million. That deal collapsed, but the same afternoon a journalist rang me to get an update on the Ward saga. I was asked how much we wanted for Ashley Ward and responded by making the point that you couldn't put a price on something you didn't want to sell, but that it was interesting to note that Dublin was valued at £4million and, in my opinion, wasn't as good as Ashley Ward. That seemed to do the trick and the following morning virtually every paper referred to the £4million-rated Ashley Ward as opposed to the £2million Ashley Ward. None of that dampened down the speculation, but eventually I took a call from the chief executive of Blackburn Rovers, John Williams, who had been authorised to make an offer to Barnsley for Ward. Their initial offer was a package worth £4million, but after some debate on 23 December 1998, a fee was agreed of £4.25million, with a further £250,000 being due based on appearances. This meant that Derby would receive a total of £600,000 guaranteed with a further £50,000 being due to them after his appearances, but it still ensured that we had made a huge profit on a player who had become a real hero at Oakwell in his brief time at the club. I wrongly assumed that Rovers and Ward had already agreed contract terms, so the following day, Christmas Eve, I rang John Williams to confirm that the deal had been completed. I nearly had a heart attack when he told me that Ward had turned down a very handsome contract offer but that they were planning further talks after the Christmas holiday. As a courtesy to our manager John Hendrie, who was busily preparing for our Boxing Day clash at Stockport County, I rang him to let him know that the Ward deal had not gone through but would probably do so in the very near future. John said that as Ward was now available to play at Stockport having recovered from injury, he would put him in the squad. For the first and only time during my career as Barnsley chairman, I interfered in team selection by telling John under no circumstances could Ward be involved at Stockport. I tried to make a joke of it by telling him that it would be a novel experience to see £4.5million being carried off on a stretcher. The Ward saga ended four days later when the player signed for Blackburn and I, like many of our fans, was very sad to see him go. However, the board and I had to take a very realistic view of running Barnsley Football Club, and turning down offers of £4.5million for one of our players was not part of our remit.

Following Ward's departure and despite the additions of Dyer and Hignett, we weren't scoring enough goals and this was reflected by the team's becalmed mid-table position. John's philosophy was to sign players who had got a track record of quality and experience, but at that time there was a young Barnsley lad earning a fine reputation for himself at Halifax Town. His name, of course, was Geoff Horsfield, who was available for £100,000. Having seen him play I felt he could make the step up but that if it didn't work out we would always be able to sell him on and get our money back. John didn't agree, feeling that he would prefer a player with a pedigree at the higher level. I was disappointed because shortly afterwards Geoff joined the Keegan revolution at Fulham, going on to have a great career with Birmingham City, Wigan Athletic and West Bromwich Albion. Some years later I bumped into Geoff at one of Barnsley FC's Player of the Year dinners. He approached me that night and asked if Barnsley had ever tried to sign him, so I told him the story. He said he'd still be interested in coming to Oakwell, but I replied: "We'd love you Geoff, but I don't suppose we'd be talking about £100,000 and £1,500 per week nowadays, would we?" His uproarious laughter and shake of the head confirmed to me that I was probably right. The Horsfield tale is one of those examples of what might have been in the recruitment of players and happens on a regular basis throughout football. For instance, towards the end of the relegation season from the Premiership we had an opportunity to sign two young Swedish stars – Freddie Ljungberg and Johan Mjallby. The combined fee would have been £500,000 and they both came highly recommended. Danny felt he needed to see them play and anyway, as it was after the transfer deadline, neither player would have been in a position to help us in our battle against relegation, his view being that he should focus all his efforts on trying to keep us in the Premier League – a perfectly understandable point of view. As we all know Ljungberg went on to sign for Arsenal, Mjallby for Celtic, and both players had wonderful careers in British football. Supporters reading this will think that we were mad for not pursuing them, but as I have researched my files for this book, I have got plenty of faxes, letters and notes from agents about many other players we did not pursue and who I've never heard of since. Our old director, Gordon Pallister, used to recount the story of how in the late 1970s the club could have signed a young John Aldridge from Newport County for £30,000, and over the years, there will have been many other opportunities of this type. But I used to console myself by looking at the deals that did come off, such as Ward, Hignett and Redfearn, and realise that things balance themselves out.

To fill the void left by Ashley Ward, John was keen to recruit another striker and became interested in signing a young Frenchman, David Zitelli, from German club Karlsruher SC. The player came highly recommended and John was keen but felt that we needed to do some more research. To that end I suggested to him that I speak to David Dein, at Arsenal, who I hoped would get me an opinion on Zitelli from a man who would certainly know all about him – the Arsenal manager Arsene Wenger. When I rang David he was actually in a meeting with his manager and handed the phone to Mr Wenger who gave me the lowdown on the player. Based on his opinion we decided not to proceed. John then turned his attention to Mike Sheron, a very gifted striker who had been a regular goalscorer for his previous two clubs, Manchester City and Stoke City. His spell at Queens Park Rangers had been less productive, so he was available for substantially less than the reported £2.75million that QPR had paid to Stoke. A complex deal was finally agreed and Sheron became a Barnsley player for a fee of £1.27million. Mike was a highly talented footballer but he never produced his best form consistently for Barnsley Football Club. With his signing we felt that there was enough quality in the squad for us to mount a serious push for the play-offs.

Sheron signed in the middle of what turned out to be an eleven match winless sequence, and although three successive victories at the end of March and in early April improved the situation, the board decided that our criteria of returning to the Premiership in the two years that we were receiving parachute payments was seriously at risk. All players signed before or during the Premiership season had signed for no more than three years, but some of the new arrivals had substantial contracts taking them beyond the end of the parachute payments. Following a dismal 3-1 home defeat to eventual champions Sunderland it was obvious that the team was going to fall some way short of our expectations and that John Hendrie should be relieved of his duties as manager. John's task had been made harder by the sales of Redfearn and Ward, but the directors had made substantial funds available to him to bring in new signings. In all fairness to John we had actually reached the sixth round of the FA Cup that season, with only a David Ginola wonder goal being the difference between us and our opponents Tottenham Hotspur. The sacking of John Hendrie was a very unpleasant task for me because he was a man I liked and a player I respected. Perhaps with hindsight the directors were a little bit premature both in appointing John in the first place and dispensing with his services in the second. That has been his one and only foray into football management so far, but he remains in the game by coaching at the Bradford City Academy and has created himself a successful career as a sports advisor to a Leeds law firm – the same firm that advised him in his contract negotiations as a player and manager.

In the February of John's season as manager, the club was proud to announce the opening of the Study Support Centre at Oakwell. The Centre was a Premier League and local government inspired initiative and was intended to offer the opportunity to children who weren't reaching their full potential at school to come and learn in the relaxed surroundings of Oakwell. The classrooms were based in the new Corner Stand and the project was launched and run by Jean Wyatt, a wonderful lady and experienced teacher whom many of her pupils will remember as fondly as I do. The official launch of the Study Support Centre did not take place until the October of 1999 when our by then highly praised Centre was to be showcased to the national media and local dignitaries, as well as the then Junior Education Minister, Redditch MP Jacqui Smith, later to become the first female Home Secretary of the United Kingdom and who achieved further notoriety in the MPs' expenses scandal. The assembled dignitaries from the Football Club and the local authority gathered in what is now the Legends' Suite at Oakwell, as did the club mascot Toby Tyke, to await the visit of the Minister. Toby's instructions were very clear – to welcome people, make them feel comfortable and generally propagate an air of goodwill. Unfortunately, when the Minister arrived, Toby took it upon himself to greet Miss Smith with rather more enthusiasm and vigour than might have been expected, and the sight of Miss Smith with her glasses askew and her hairdo ruined as she attempted to retain her dignity in the face of Toby's assault is a picture that remains with me to this day. I remember remarking to Michael Spinks that I doubted whether Miss Smith had entered politics to be ragged by a big furry animal. I'm pleased to say that the

Study Support Centre managed to survive that incident and continues to flourish to this day.

Towards the end of the promotion season of 1996-97, the board had started to plan the development of the north end of the stadium and the land behind it. The development would comprise a modern youth academy to meet the criteria laid down in the FA's Charter for Quality document as promoted by Howard Wilkinson, and it was further proposed that a new 6,000-seater stand should be sited on the old Spion Kop end, which would house all of the professional and academy requirements for offices, dressing rooms, medical rooms and staff canteen. We further needed to replace the club's matchday police control room with a much more sophisticated structure. The total cost of the whole development was likely to top £4.5million. As part of this ambitious project, a figure of £275,000 was agreed by the club to buy the old Co-op sports ground, which was adjacent to Oakwell and by further increasing the size of our own Queen's Ground, we then had the space to proceed with the academy (my predecessor Geoff Buckle had agreed a deal to buy that same piece of land in the 1980s for £40,000 but the old Co-op committee in Barnsley vetoed the deal). Part of the funding for this project, as well as the landscaping of the East Stand car park and Grove Street car park, came from an organisation called City Challenge, who on the basis that we would sell them the unused part of our landholding behind the East Stand, which abutted Pontefract Road, for a figure of £325,000, they would then provide us with a grant of £800,000. We borrowed a further £2million from our bankers, with the balance being funded through our own resources. This development began during John Hendrie's era and was completed during season 1999-2000, with the indoor academy football arena following a year later. By the time this development was complete, Barnsley Football Club had a facility that was the envy of many clubs throughout the country and is unique in that it is adjacent to the club's main stadium. On completion of the development it attracted enormous attention from others clubs, both in the United Kingdom and in Europe, who visited Oakwell to see for themselves what had been achieved and what ideas they could take away. Our academy was intended to be much more than just football coaching, and to that end we appointed Peter Caskin, a retired headteacher, who had for many years worked for the Barnsley Schools FA, as our academy director. Former player Mark Smith was appointed Under 19 manager, with another former Red, Colin Walker, managing the Under 17s. The academy and North Stand development were seen by the directors as a legacy from our journey to the Premier League and was a further sign of our growing involvement in the community as it became a focal point for many young people and their families in the town.

CHAPTER 11

So Near Yet So Far

E ric Winstanley once more took over the reins as caretaker manager as the now familiar search for a new boss was underway. He steered the team to a seven-point harvest from his three games in charge, with the season ending with Barnsley finishing in a very disappointing thirteenth position in the table. Many names were linked with the job, but those of Dave Bassett, Steve Bruce and our former player Mick McCarthy were of the greatest interest to the board. It had been becoming increasingly difficult to find a suitable location to meet potential candidates for private discussions because the rumour mill around town was always full of stories that such and such a manager had been seen leaving Oakwell or having dinner with me at Ardsley House. Clearly it would have been ridiculous to select such a public venue for such secretive talks. Therefore, I adopted the habit of meeting potential candidates just off Junction 36 of the M1, who would then follow me to my own house nearby. That summer Steve Bruce, who I'd met some years earlier through his friendship with our old manager Mel Machin, was the first of those to visit my home. In Steve's case he was torn between ourselves and Huddersfield Town, but decided to take up the challenge in West Yorkshire. I then met Mick McCarthy who was, at the time, the manager of the Republic of Ireland. He would have been a great choice and in view of the fact that he had formed the impression that the Irish FA would not be offering him a new contract, he was a strong candidate. The following week, I was disappointed to get a call from Mick telling me that the Irish FA had offered him a new, improved contract and that he had chosen to accept it. Next in the frame was David Moyes who had steered Preston North End to the Division Three play-off final that year. A discreet enquiry through his agent indicated that Moyes would be interested in the Barnsley job but wasn't in a position to make a decision until after the end of the play-off campaign. The Barnsley board were not in a position to wait until the end of May, so we turned our attention to Dave Bassett. 'Harry', as he was widely known in football, was a highly respected and successful football club manager who had a number of promotions on his CV. He was, at the time, unattached, and the discussion I had with Dave that day was very encouraging. He had done his homework on Barnsley Football Club in general and our squad in particular, and I'd no hesitation in recommending to my directors that he should be given the post. We were all well aware that Dave Bassett wouldn't have quite the universal appeal to our fans as some of the other candidates, partly because of his Bramall Lane connections and also because of his so-called style of football. But given our criteria of having one final push, aided by our last parachute payment, at a second promotion to the Premiership, we decided to offer Bassett the job on the basis of his very strong CV and excellent interview.

There was never a dull moment when Dave Bassett was the manager of Barnsley Football Club. Given the brief of challenging for promotion, his style of football was flamboyant and full of surprises, particularly in his first season. Results could be unpredictable, never more so than the last weekend of August, when on the Saturday we'd comfortably beaten Portsmouth 6-0 but went down 6-1 at Ipswich on the Bank Holiday Monday. As an aside, Barry Taylor and I had been out to dinner the previous night with our old friend David Sheepshanks, the Ipswich chairman, and some of his board members. It'd been a long and somewhat boozy evening and we found ourselves a little bit short of transport on the way back from dinner on the Suffolk coast. I recall that Mr Sheepshanks was the one delegated to make the journey back in the boot of the car. By 5pm the following day I'm sure David's hangover was far less than painful than mine.

As is the case with all new managers, Harry declared that the squad needed strengthening and felt that experienced and trusted recruits were necessary if we were to mount a serious promotion challenge. Midfielder Geoff Thomas was signed on a free transfer from Nottingham Forest and goalkeeper Kevin Miller also joined from struggling Crystal Palace. Palace were in administration and needed to sell players, so at the £250,000 that we paid Miller was thought to be a bargain and a suitable replacement for David Watson. David's career had been shattered by a serious knee injury that had manifested itself in the previous season and despite innovative surgery in an attempt to cure the problem, he was no longer able to withstand the demands of professional football. David has carved out for himself a great career as a goalkeeping coach and is tipped to become part of the England set-up in the future. Bassett also brought to the club experienced central defender David Tuttle from Crystal Palace for £125,000, highly rated full-back John Curtis arrived on loan from Manchester United, and another experienced centre half, Steve Chettle, signed from Nottingham Forest. Bassett's major signing was that of Neil Shipperley. Although Harry was blessed with the strike resources of Dyer and Sheron, as well as the creativity of Hignett, he wanted a big man to play up front, so swooped for Shipperley, with whom he'd worked at Nottingham Forest. Forest's sales were being handled by a firm of agents called First Artists and I eventually agreed a deal with their director, Phil Smith to bring Shipperley to Barnsley for £700,000. Smith had been originally looking for in excess of £1 million but after getting stuck on £800,000 for a day or two, he was able to recommend to the powers that be at Forest that they take Barnsley's bid. I was rather surprised and angry when some weeks later First Artists sent us an invoice for a substantial sum for their services rendered. In a somewhat heated discussion with Mr Smith, I pointed out to him that it had been me working for Barnsley, not him, and that we didn't owe them a penny. Eventually, to avoid the potential for unpleasant and very public legal action, it was decided to make a small payment to First Artists in full and final settlement of their claim against us. We heard no more from them about the matter.

This tale perhaps illustrates the growing influence and activities of agents that I had witnessed from my early days of being chairman of Barnsley Football Club. I used to find it odd that football club officials who knew each other well would choose to deal with a middleman rather than speaking directly to their counterparts at other clubs. However, the game was changing and you couldn't pretend that this wasn't happening. I did, and do, believe that there is a place for agents in the game, and they can provide support and protection for young footballers who are not always in a position to be able to handle their own negotiations. In every walk of life there are good and not so good characters and in the world of football agents, whilst the balance might be slightly different, the same truism applies. There were many tales of dodgy agents offering illegal payments to managers, chief executives and scouts, but many of these stories were unprovable. I remember discussing the situation many times with Graham Bean, the FA Compliance Officer at that time and former detective at Barnsley CID. It was Graham's job to root out such irregularities, but as in most aspects of criminality, knowing it and proving it are two very different things. As a chairman who by this stage of his career was expected to handle most of the club's transfer negotiations, I was only once offered a blatant bribe, although on other occasions there were subtle suggestions as to what may have been possible. On the occasion to which I refer I had met an agent at Tankersley Manor one afternoon and we were discussing one of his players whom our manager wanted to sign. We had held quite lengthy discussions, which had not gone very far, when the clearly frustrated agent put his pen down and said that we hadn't even discussed his fee yet, so if we would agree to a £30,000 payment to him, he would give me £15,000 cash in return and as long as the player was given a slightly improved contract then all the details that I was trying to hammer out could be left to me. I was somewhat taken aback by what I'd heard and in hindsight I would probably have been wise to abandon the deal and go home. Instead, I told the guy that I would ignore what he'd just said and that I would continue to negotiate the player's contract in a proper way, although he would not be getting any fee at all. I'd love to name and shame the agent concerned, but because this was a one on one conversation, I am not in a position to substantiate these facts.

As season 1999-2000 under Bassett progressed, goals flowed in abundance and although we scored plenty, we leaked plenty as well. The Barnsley supporters slowly started to warm to their new manager, although some of his selection decisions, which almost always turned out to be very astute, did tend to surprise and confuse on a regular basis. By November we looked on track to achieve our ambition of a top six finish, but as ever in football there was a cloud on the horizon. This came in the guise of press speculation linking Harry to the vacant manager's job at Blackburn Rovers. After the home game against Birmingham on 20 November, Harry told me that he'd had an unofficial approach from Blackburn and that because of their financial firepower the job had some attraction. He explained that wherever he had been in his career he had always been expected to operate on a shoestring budget, so this would be an opportunity for him to experience a different aspect of football management. He also gave an indication of what they were prepared to pay him, which was an awful lot more than he was on at Barnsley. The board had authorised me to take whatever reasonable steps I could to convince Bassett to stay and this wasn't as difficult as I had feared because in his heart of hearts he was a loyal man who enjoyed his work at Barnsley and respected the faith that we had shown in giving him the job. We agreed that the board would, from time to time when finances allowed, make small one-off bonus payments to him and he, being satisfied with what was being suggested, took the Blackburn approach no further. Being the professional that he was, that little hiccough had no impact on Dave's work and after a 5-1 demolition of Blackburn at Oakwell towards the end of January, things were looking promising. A patchy run then undermined our promotion push and with three games remaining it was clear that whilst we hadn't done enough to achieve our ultimate ambition of an automatic promotion place, we were certain of landing a play-off spot. With eighty-eight goals scored and sixty-seven conceded, it had been a rollercoaster season, but Dave Bassett had shrewdly harnessed the talents of his creative players and the bigger stronger athletes – the type of player with whom he had usually been associated with. Our final league position was a very creditable fourth, but that meant that we had a very daunting first leg semi-final tie at St Andrews, Birmingham, waiting for us.

Having lost 3-1 in the regular league season at St Andrews, we travelled with some trepidation and once again the manager sprang another surprise with his team selection that afternoon, picking Robin van der Laan up front to partner Neil Shipperley. Fate took a hand when van der Laan was injured, being replaced by Geoff Thomas. Shipperley had scored an early goal, giving us a 1-0 lead going into the interval, during which Dave Bassett made an inspired substitution that was to turn the game in our favour. Bruce Dyer replaced Geoff Thomas and started to repay a big chunk of his transfer fee by notching two goals to put us on our way to a famous victory. Hignett plundered another, and we drove back up the motorway having outplayed and deservedly beaten the Birmingham City of Trevor Francis 4-0. The second leg at Oakwell on the Thursday evening was a bit of a non-event, and although we lost 2-1 with Dyer once again finding the net, it didn't really matter because for the first time in the history of Barnsley Football Club we were on our way to the twin towers of Wembley.

Our opponents for the 1999-2000 Division One Play Off Final were to be Ipswich Town, who had humiliated us 6-1 at Portman Road earlier in the season and then completed the double over us with a 2-0 victory at Oakwell in February. It was obviously going to be a very stern test. Once again excitement and anticipation flooded through the town and more than 30,000 tickets were snapped up by Barnsley fans, who were eagerly anticipating a big day out at Wembley. Club staff were inundated, not just by the demand for tickets but also by the need for merchandise. The manager and his staff were doing their best to protect the players from all of the hype and publicity and decided to head off to London a few days before the big game on the Bank Holiday Monday, 29 May. The directors and their families decided to travel to Wembley by coach on the morning of the game, leaving Barnsley at 9am. As we drove down the M1 it was exhilarating and heartwarming to see the Barnsley traffic heading off to Wembley. I was as tense and nervous as I'd ever been on a trip to a Barnsley game because I, and all of my directors, knew that the immediate future of Barnsley Football Club hinged on the result of that one match. If we had beaten Ipswich, we would have been promoted and would have had at least one more year of Premiership football to look forward to in addition to two more years of parachute payments. But if we lost the match, it was inevitable that having come to the end of our parachute payments, cost cutting and downsizing would be the order of the day. On arrival at Wembley we headed for the Banqueting Suite, where there was a reception and luncheon laid on for the officials of both competing clubs, FA and Football League representatives, special guests and so-called celebrity supporters. I took my place at the top table, but was finding the tension almost unbearable so didn't really enjoy the meal very much. Although I was supposed to be exchanging pleasantries with our counterparts from Ipswich and other guests at the luncheon, I wasn't really much in the mood for that, so decided to use the special pass that I'd been given, which allowed me access to all areas of the great Wembley Stadium, to go down to the dressing room to see the manager and the players to wish them well – a ritual that I followed before every Barnsley game, also paying a visit to the dressing room after each match to offer either commiserations or congratulations. Having done that, it was back to the Banqueting Suite for a few minutes before taking my seat on the front row of the Royal Box. It was both gratifying and humbling to see so many Barnsley fans at Wembley that day. My final act before the kick-off was to reach across and shake hands with my old friend David Sheepshanks, the Ipswich Chairman, to wish him well, and he offered reciprocal good wishes. Whilst it was done with a smile on our faces, neither of us meant it and I'm sure we'd have slit each other's throats if that's what it took to get our club promoted that day.

For the final time that season, Dave Bassett sprang a surprise when he opted to leave Nicky Eaden on the bench in favour of on-loan John Curtis, who took the right-back spot. It was common knowledge, by that stage, that John was likely to be joining Blackburn rather than Barnsley in the summer and I had hoped that Nicky would get the nod. The game started brightly and so did we, taking the lead on six minutes with a Craig Hignett thunderbolt from twenty-five yards. Some claim it was a Richard Wright own goal, as it bounced off the bar before hitting the Ipswich keeper and going in the net, but I'm not having that – Hignett scored and it was 1-0 Barnsley. Having taken that early lead, we were then unable to press home our advantage and a Tony Mowbray equaliser just before the half hour mark rocked us back on our heels. But on the stroke of half-time, there occurred a seminal moment in that game and possibly in the history of Barnsley Football Club. It came about when we were awarded a penalty after Ipswich keeper Wright had brought down the irrepressible Hignett. Up stepped Darren Barnard, whose trusty left foot had already successfully converted five spot kicks that season. Darren's penalty was far from the worst I've ever seen, but the big Ipswich keeper dived to his right and palmed the ball away from goal. The half-time break quickly followed and as the game re-started it seemed clear that we were a bit flat and that Ipswich had gained inspiration from the heroics of their keeper. In all honesty, even the most biased Barnsley fan would have to admit that we were second best for most of the second half and a goal from Richard Naylor followed six minutes later by another from Marcus Stewart, a player who had been a pain in our backside both for Ipswich and Huddersfield Town, saw us trailing 3-1. We looked out of it, but still created opportunities. Wright then somehow scooped out a Georgi Hristov header and although a Hignett penalty on seventy-eight minutes restored our belief, a late Martijn Reuser strike saw Ipswich on their way to the Premiership.

Whoever coined the old adage that Wembley is not a place for losers was absolutely right, as I felt devastated at the final whistle. On the face of it, it had been a terrific match played in great spirit to the backdrop of a wonderful atmosphere created by two sets of fans who were fiercely proud of their own team yet appreciative of the opposition and of the occasion. However, I couldn't help feeling utterly deflated at this defeat, but as chairman I had to maintain my poise and offered my congratulations to Mr Sheepshanks and his colleagues on the Ipswich board. I then had to endure the Wembley tradition of a victorious team taking the long walk up the steps and along the Royal Box to be awarded their medals. I regret to say that I found it difficult to shake the hands of every member of the Ipswich squad, managing only to congratulate a small number of the winning team. I did greet their manager, George Burley – a man I'd got to know quite well over the years – with as much grace as I could possibly muster. The next Wembley custom that I had to endure was an after-match reception where I once again had to put on a brave face and mouth more pleasantries to well-meaning acquaintances when all I wanted to do was get on the bus and go home. My spirits were lifted briefly as we walked down the Wembley steps back to the car park where we were greeted by a band of Ipswich fans who warmly wished us well and thanked us for our contribution to what they described as a wonderful day – it might have been for them but it wasn't for us. The atmosphere on the directors' coach was very gloomy as we fought our way through the crowds back to the M1, although one or two of my colleagues cheered themselves up by opening a couple of bottles of the champagne that we had taken with us in anticipation of a celebration. By the time we'd reached Leicester Forest East I had barely spoken a word, but I finally broke my silence to tell Christianne that having thought long and hard about my position as chairman, it was probably time for me to step down from that role and from the Board of Directors of Barnsley Football Club. Her response was that it wasn't the time to be making major decisions and that I ought to consider the situation in a less highly charged atmosphere. Over the following few days I thought long and hard about my position but decided to stay on because I did not want to be seen as a quitter and because I still thought I had a lot to offer. In hindsight, it probably wouldn't have been a bad time for me to have walked away because perhaps that day at Wembley had taken more out of me than I realised.

Whilst the play-off system has been a great success for the Football League and has created huge excitement as well as huge revenues, the great disadvantage for clubs involved in the play-offs is that it shortens their close season hugely. With the finals not being held until the end of May and managers typically going on holiday immediately afterwards, it generally means that clubs can only start finalising their plans for the following season in the middle of June. After Wembley, Dave Bassett flew to Spain for a fortnight's well earned break, but on his return, requested a private meeting with me at which he, out of the blue, offered his resignation. His rationale was that the club would be operating in more straightened circumstances and that he would understand if we felt that we needed to bring a manager in at less cost to the club. The view of the board and myself was that Dave's experience of working on a shoestring budget and with his vast array of contacts throughout the football world to help recruit players was going to be vital in our quest to remain competitive in the First Division. With that in mind, Dave's offer of resignation was turned down. We then set about the task of re-shaping the squad and an early departure that summer was Craig Hignett, who signed for Blackburn Rovers for £2.25million. This was no surprise to me because some months earlier, as the club was focusing on its promotion battle there had been much speculation over Hignett's future. One particular article in the *Yorkshire Post* had really irritated me by suggesting that Hignett was on his way to Bradford City. I rang the reporter concerned and made it very clear to him that Hignett was not for sale because our only focus was on getting promoted. However, unwisely, I then went on to add that even if he was to leave Barnsley, I couldn't imagine him going to a 'small club' like Bradford City. I ought to have known better because my remarks were printed verbatim the following morning. It was not any great surprise when later that day my old friend Geoffrey Richmond, the City Chairman, called me to let me know, in very strong terms, what he thought of what I'd said. I responded in similar vein and although we exchanged further insults, that bust-up didn't affect our friendship. After that incident, I was confident that the Hignett speculation would die the death, but his agent, Struan Marshall, who had helped engineer his move to Barnsley in the first place, had picked up on the rumours and sniffed a deal for his player. I made it clear to Struan that Hignett was going nowhere, but that we would review the situation when we knew where we were at the end of the season. Soon after our defeat at Wembley, Struan was back on the phone to me to remind me of the conversation, and very soon

Hignett became the target for Fulham and Blackburn Rovers. Both clubs were prepared to match our valuation of £2million, but we managed to squeeze an extra £250,000 out of Blackburn Rovers for the player's signature. I was then to be surprised and disappointed when the manager recommended to the board that new contracts be offered to Eric Tinkler, Robin van der Laan and Geoff Thomas. My view was that younger and more mobile midfield players were what we should have been seeking but, to my regret, we agreed to continue our policy of backing the manager with his recommendations, and the three of them re-signed. Young full-back Carl Regan was signed on for £10,000 from Everton, striker Lee Jones joined from Wrexham, with a young Alex Neil signing from Airdrie. With youngsters such as Anthony Kay, Chris Barker and Brian O'Callaghan coming through the ranks, Dave Bassett thought that he had a competitive squad.

The 2000-01 season started with a home game against Norwich City and with Carl Regan marking his debut with an early red card, our performance needed to be committed and solid, which it was. Another debutant that day, Lee Jones, got his name on the scoresheet to force a hard earned 1-0 win. A run of poor results then followed, culminating in a 5-1 hammering at Fulham one Sunday afternoon, where a young Louis Saha was outstanding for the home team. To make matters worse I got food poisoning from some dodgy quiche and my journey back up the M1 was punctuated by regular visits to service stations. By December, results were giving cause for concern and the board and I felt that clear the air talks with the manager would be appropriate. Bassett understood the position perfectly and after seeking assurances from myself that he would be given enough time to turn things around – assurances that I was not in a position to give – it was agreed that we would part company. Dave Bassett during his time at Barnsley had, on more than one occasion, shown his loyalty to the club, and his departure was equally as gracious, agreeing to a very reasonable compromise in respect of the compensation that he should have been due to. He arrived at Oakwell relatively unloved by Barnsley fans and, somewhat unfairly, left on a similar note.

CHAPTER 12

Spackman

The departure of Dave Bassett prompted the usual frenzy of interest in the vacant manager's job at Barnsley with the mix of applications coming from well known names in football and the traditional quota of cranks and lunatics. The field narrowed itself down quite quickly in the eyes of the board into three favourites – Dave Jones, Nigel Spackman and Jan Molby. My own favoured choice would have been Steve Bruce, but Steve was considered unacceptable by other board members, partly because he had once turned us down and partly because of his connections with Huddersfield Town and Sheffield United. Jan Molby, then the manager of Kidderminster Harriers, was interviewed at my house, although the element of secrecy with which I liked to conduct these matters was somewhat undermined when Jan turned up in his club sponsored car with his name and the name of the sponsors emblazoned in bright red letters. Jan interviewed well, but was a quieter and more understated man than I had remembered from his brief loan spell at Oakwell in Danny Wilson's second season. Nigel Spackman came with an impressive CV and a reputation as one of the game's up and coming young coaches. He had enjoyed a successful stint managing Sheffield United but resigned from his position at Bramall Lane in protest at his board selling a number of his key players without consultation – Jan Aage Fjortoft being one of them. The board's preferred option was Dave Jones, who had done a marvellous job at Stockport County before enhancing his reputation at Southampton. He had been infamously suspended and sacked from his role at Southampton following completely unfounded criminal allegations made against him. Dave was excellent in interview and both the vice-chairman and I decided that we'd take it upon ourselves to offer him the job there and then. We thought we had got our man but he was reluctant to finally commit himself that afternoon, feeling that he needed to go away to discuss things with his family, understandably, but promised to give us an answer within the next couple of days. It turned out that he was due to meet the board of Wolverhampton Wanderers in London the following day and ironically I was to discover some years later that as he was coming out of his interview, our former manager Dave Bassett was going in. Dave Jones was then offered the Wolves job and it was on New Year's Eve, 2000 when he rang me to give the bad news. He seemed genuinely sorry to have turned us down, so with that in mind, a couple of years later when one evening I was at a function at Brooklands Hotel, I discovered that Wolves were staying there prior to their game at Oakwell the next day, so sent Dave a bottle of champagne with my compliments. Nigel Spackman then became the board's unanimous choice. A further meeting with Nigel was arranged at my home, terms were agreed and the former Chelsea and Liverpool midfielder became the next Barnsley manager, the sixth full-time manager with whom I had worked since becoming chairman. His appointment appeared to be universally popular amongst the Oakwell faithful and the board's very simple brief to Nigel that January was to ensure that we didn't get relegated that season.

Nigel Spackman's brief managerial reign at Barnsley had very inauspicious beginnings. His first match in charge saw a 3-2 defeat against Birmingham City and although the style of football improved markedly under Nigel, it wasn't until his sixth game that we picked up our first victory with a 1-0 home win against Crystal Palace. The Palace game was the beginning of a remarkable run of results, which saw us achieve seven wins from nine games, with the tenth game of the sequence being a 1-1 draw against Wimbledon. That spell of excellent form took us comfortably into mid-table with fifty-four points earned and four games to play. Perhaps those last four matches should have been seen by the board as something of a warning because we gained no points, scored one goal and conceded ten. Nonetheless, the manager had achieved his primary target as we comfortably avoided relegation by six points.

In helping him to preserve our First Division status, the board authorised the manager to make a number of signings. Bradford City striker Isaiah Rankin was the first of these, who cost £300,000, with midfielder Steve Hayward signing the following day from Fulham for £35,000. Burly defender Lee Crooks, a Wakefield lad, was signed from Manchester City for £40,000 despite suffering from a knee injury. The board and I were assured that Lee would soon be ready for first team action, but that proved not to be the case as Lee didn't make his debut for the Reds until the start of the following season. Goalkeeper Andy Marriott also came in as back-up to Kevin Miller. The manager also made recommendations to reshape the backroom staff at Oakwell, with most of Bassett's men either having left when Dave did or who were deemed not to be suitable by Nigel. The vastly experienced Derek Fazackerley was brought in as first team coach. Fazackerley had a long and impressive career as a player with Blackburn Rovers before embarking on his career as a coach. Since leaving Oakwell he has worked closely with Sven Goran Eriksson with England, Manchester City and Leicester City. Legendary Liverpool striker Ian Rush also came to Barnsley, holding a couple of sessions each week with the club's strikers. Again, this was a progressive move by Spackman, although Rush's obvious striking prowess never seemed to rub off on our front men. Nigel also expressed a wish to bring in a new physiotherapist, a man named Jim Webb with whom Nigel had worked at Chelsea. Jim had very modern ideas on the role of the physiotherapist at a football club and he implemented a diet and fitness regime that reflected these progressive ideas. Although Jim's knowledge and approach to the job seemed very impressive, I suspect that many of our players did not buy into this new regime and were far happier with the approach that you might expect from a traditional football club physio. History also shows that injured players during that era seemed to spend far longer re-gaining full match fitness than one might have expected. The contrast between

Spackman's regime and Bassett's was stark indeed. Nigel had his more modern approach, whilst Harry loved nothing better than getting the lads together for a Chinese meal and a few beers and allowing them to let their hair down.

The most distasteful recommendation made by the manager to the board during the re-shaping of his backroom staff was when it was suggested that there was no longer a place for Eric Winstanley at the Football Club. Nigel wanted his own men in place and reluctantly, in line with our traditional policy of supporting a manager where possible, it fell to me to undertake one of the most unpleasant tasks that I had to carry out during my entire stint as chairman, which was to tell Eric that he was surplus to requirements at his beloved Barnsley Football Club – his hometown club with whom he'd had a wonderful career as a legend of a player, a great coach and a loyal servant both to the club and to myself and my father personally. With heavy heart I ended Eric Winstanley's association with Barnsley Football Club.

Having flirted with relegation the previous season, hopes were high after a full pre-season that Nigel Spackman, with a re-shaped squad, could take us to the upper reaches of the First Division. This would have to be achieved, though, without star striker and fans' favourite Neil Shipperley, who had expressed a desire to move back to the London area. After a long chat with the player it was clear that nothing would change his mind so he was sold to Wimbledon for £750,000. Nigel brought in a number of reinforcements to the squad that summer, notably Kevin Donovan from Grimsby Town, who Nigel saw as a replacement for the now-departed Martin Bullock, and Dean Gorre arrived from Huddersfield Town. Clearly, the loss of Shipperley meant that Nigel had to improve his striking options and he plumped to sign Kevin Gallen, also from Huddersfield Town. Another memorable signing by Nigel that summer was that of Kevin Dixon, a young midfielder from Leeds United with whom the manager had worked within the England Under 18 squad. As a measure of Dixon's success at Barnsley, he never made a first team appearance.

We had an awful start to the season taking a 4-0 thumping from Bradford City before getting off the mark with a sketchy 2-1 home win against Nottingham Forest the following week. Our next fixture saw us away at Gillingham on an extremely hot and humid late August day. The whole experience seemed surreal because we must have had eighty per cent of possession but barely had a shot on goal. Defensively, we were unable to cope with their more direct style and we lost the game 3-0. On the long drive back that evening, myself and my colleagues, who had travelled with me in my car, genuinely couldn't work out whether we were a decent side who passed the ball well but were short of firepower or were just a tippy-tappy outfit, all show and no substance. We were soon to found out because a ghastly run culminating in a 3-1 defeat at Sheffield Wednesday saw us pick up only two wins during that period. If the alarm bells weren't ringing at the end of the previous season, that night at Hillsborough ensured that they were there for all to hear. The future of the manager had been discussed by the directors earlier during the bad run of results. Not only were concerns expressed about results and performances, but his transfer policy was also the source of some worry. What particularly perturbed the board was the manager's signing of midfielder Peter Sand, twin brother of Danish legend Ebbe Sand. The fact that Sand clearly wasn't good enough for the First Division was almost incidental to the fact that the manager wanted to sign another midfielder when it was clear that he hadn't adequately replaced the now departed Shipperley. Immediately after the Hillsborough humiliation, as the Barnsley directors gathered in the visitor's boardroom to discuss the situation, any experienced boardroom watcher would have seen the signs that there was trouble afoot. I canvassed the views of my colleagues, who were emphatically and unanimously of the view that Spackman and his number two, Fazackerley, should be relieved of their posts as soon as was practical. I arranged to meet both men at Oakwell the following day to do so. Because of the dire performances and results and poor balance in the squad, Spackman's dismissal was inevitable and was the least anguished over and the least emotional parting of the ways over which I had ever presided. Glynn Hodges, Reserve Team coach and a rare survivor from the Bassett era, was asked to step into the breach as caretaker manager, and he got off to a winning start by dint of a 3-2 scoreline over West Bromwich Albion at Oakwell.

In the past, the Board of Directors of Barnsley Football Club had built a reputation for loyalty to its managers and I'm disappointed that this changed in my era. However, directors of a football club are in the difficult position of having to achieve the balance between stability and ambition. When things are going badly a judgement call has to be made as to whether it's a short-term blip or a long-term decline. The implications behind staying with a manager in whom you are losing faith can be very far reaching and it very quickly boils down to a very simple choice – either back him or sack him. In the case of Barnsley Football Club it must be remembered that in my era the directors saw it as their responsibility to create the best conditions possible for the manager to do his job and not to try and do the job for the manager. If the board showed misplaced loyalty to a particular manager they could find themselves in a position of authorising player transfers that are clearly wrong for the club – as evidenced by the signing of Peter Sand and others by Nigel Spackman. Of course, a poor choice of manager in the first place inevitably means that the life span of that manager is going to be relatively short.

CHAPTER 13

The Slippery Slope

Following the sacking of Nigel Spackman, a directors' meeting was held at my home to discuss both the vacant manager's position and the overall issues surrounding the club. The general view of the other members of the board was that instead of the by now traditional method of us going about selecting a manager, which until that time had involved myself and sometimes the vice-chairman in conducting the interview process, a sub-committee of the board should be established. I have to confess to some disappointment at this proposal because it suggested to me that the trust and confidence that I always enjoyed amongst my colleagues had been somewhat eroded. But other than resigning, I had little option but to accept the democratic view of the other directors. I suppose that given the spiral of decline into which we had entered, it should have been no surprise to me that their faith in me had been somewhat shaken. The meeting also discussed the club's financial position, which would have been seriously jeopardised were we to be relegated.

The managerial selection sub-committee, consisting of myself, Barry Taylor, Mick Hayselden and John Kelly, began its work by sifting through the long list of those who had expressed interest in the job. The names of Steve Cotterill, Nicky Law and Steve Parkin came to the fore. Having taken soundings from a number of people about these three men, notably Howard Wilkinson who was the Chairman of the League Managers' Association, it was decided by the committee to make contact with Steve Parkin and Nicky Law. Law, a former Barnsley player, had been very successful under trying circumstances at Chesterfield, where he was aided by another ex-Red, Ian Banks. Both men were invited to my house for an interview and they both came across very well. Unofficial approaches had been made to Rochdale manager Steve Parkin. Steve had cut his managerial teeth at Mansfield Town before taking over at Rochdale and was very well regarded by his employers. Steve was also interviewed that Sunday morning at my house and his shining determination and down to earth approach just gave him the edge over Nicky Law. The committee unanimously decided that, if it were possible to prise Parkin away from Rochdale, then it was believed he would be the ideal man for the Oakwell job and the challenge that it presented. I made formal contact with Rochdale, but their Chairman, David Kilpatrick, someone whom I had come to know quite well over the years, rebuffed our first enquiry. David also made it clear to me that in future discussions I needed to speak to the Rochdale Finance Director, Graham Morris. In my conversations with Mr Morris it became very clear that Rochdale would fight tooth and nail to hang on to their manager. They were also aware that Steve would probably want to bring his assistant, Tony Ford, to Barnsley with him. The whole compensation issue became quite messy and although Steve took up his duties at Oakwell in the mid-November of 2001, a settlement between Barnsley and Rochdale was not agreed until a Football League Tribunal adjudicated on the matter in March 2002, at which we were ordered to pay Rochdale £130,000 as compensation for them losing Parkin and Ford.

Much like his predecessor Nigel Spackman, Steve Parkin's brief when he stepped into the Oakwell hot seat was to get us away from the drop zone. The first match with Steve at the helm was at home to Wimbledon, which was drawn 1-1, but two away defeats at Norwich City and Wolves quickly followed. The board's policy of attempting to support the manager in the transfer market resulted in us accepting Steve's recommendation to sign midfielder Gary Jones from his old club Rochdale. Jones had an excellent debut as we comprehensively beat Sheffield Wednesday 3-0 at Oakwell in a televised game on Sunday evening, 2 December – it seems strange to talk about league football on a Sunday night, but that was an experiment that ITV Digital had hoped would bring them enhanced viewing figures. As a measure of how well Jones had played that evening, many fans left Oakwell comparing Gary to all-time favourite Neil Redfearn. What a shame that he didn't live up to those early expectations. Six days later an impressive 4-1 home win over Walsall set us on our way, and after those two encouraging victories we then proceeded to go on a further ten match unbeaten run. In the transfer market Parkin also made permanent the signing of Chris Lumsdon, a highly talented midfield player who had initially been on loan from Sunderland. The unbeaten run eventually came to an end in an unfortunate 1-0 defeat away to Birmingham. The team had played well that day and with Mike Sheron hitting the bar and Chris Morgan going close with a couple of headers, we were extremely unlucky not to get anything from the game. I spoke to Steve that evening and he was bitterly disappointed and apologetic for the loss, but I told him it was just one of those things and that he needed to lift his spirits and get things back on track the following week at Coventry. The match at Coventry began disastrously when a mistake by Chris Morgan let the home side in for a simple first goal. The afternoon didn't get any better and we were comprehensively beaten 4-0. The following week's home match against Crystal Palace proved equally as disastrous where, once again, we lost heavily – this time suffering a 4-1 reverse. Those three defeats were part of a sequence that saw us collect only two points from a possible twenty-one, and although victories over Watford and Preston North End, sandwiched by defeat at the Hawthorns, gave us some hope, it was clear that we were in serious danger of being relegated. By this stage the transfer deadline had been and gone and the board had sanctioned three further signings – Kevin Betsy, a winger from Fulham, vastly experienced centre-half Mike Flynn, from Stockport County, and left-back Paul Gibbs, who was brought in on a free transfer from Brentford. Additionally, the directors had rejected an opportunistic £500,000 offer from West Bromwich Albion for star striker Bruce Dyer. Not only was the offer so low it was derisory, it was felt that selling our leading goal scorer would have been utter madness given the predicament we found ourselves in.

With three matches left we still had an opportunity to save ourselves, but the first of these assignments was away at Maine Road to face highflying, free scoring Manchester City, who would go on to be runaway champions. We suffered a shattering 5-1 defeat as the Kevin Keegan inspired Blues tore us apart. It pains me to say it, but we looked a dispirited, dejected sorry bunch that day and only victory the following Saturday against Norwich City at Oakwell would give us any hope of salvation. On a personal note, the week before the Norwich game was very difficult for myself and my family. My father-in-law was suddenly taken very ill on the Thursday evening and by the time the paramedics had got him to Barnsley Hospital he was pronounced dead. It fell to me to formally identify the body and, having spent most of the night comforting my wife and mother-in-law, I went off to work briefly before spending the rest of the day with my family dealing with the formalities that such an event demands. By match day, I was in something of a daze, having barely slept for two days. Having gone through my usual match day customs, I settled into my seat in the directors' box fully expecting to see a performance from our team of grit, determination and endeavour. That turned out not to be the case and it was embarrassing, humiliating and scarcely believable the way that a Barnsley team should subside so meekly in such an important fixture. The game, which was played out to a growing crescendo of protests aimed at myself and the board, was lost 2-0, with that score and results elsewhere condemning Barnsley Football Club to the third tier of English football for the first time since 1979. The protests continued long after the final whistle, but in truth they were wasting their breath because I didn't need reminding of how low we had sunk. Eventually I found sufficient strength and energy to go and face the media and made the typically defiant utterances that those circumstances demand. But I suspect that my show in front of the media that day was the least convincing performance I'd ever given during my time as chairman. That disastrous season at least ended on a high note with a 1-0 away victory at Wimbledon signing off our First Division status.

Over the years I have thought long and hard as to what changed so quickly under Steve Parkin's managership. He was a hardworking, committed manager who put his all into getting success for Barnsley Football Club. Fans might laugh and say that we had bad payers, but that same set of lads had gone on a twelve match unbeaten run and looked like turning the season around. To this day it remains a mystery to me how the team's form collapsed in such a short space of time, although as a contributory factor it had emerged that there was what was commonly referred to as a 'drinking culture' at Oakwell. In all honesty, the participants in these activities were mainly younger players at the Football Club but the club did not deal with the situation at all well. I recollect one incident from that time when one May Saturday afternoon after relegation had been confirmed, I had an appointment in town. As I walked down Shambles Street I recognised five of our young players sitting on the pavement outside what is now Walkabout having a few drinks. They clearly saw me and as I came out from my appointment they were no longer there. But I had a pretty good idea of where they were likely to be, so I nipped down the Arcade and up through the ginnel next to Frank Bird's Menswear to find the same five wannabee footballers continuing their beery Saturday afternoon. Clearly, as it was the close season and it was their own time and their own careers they were playing with, I could do little other than to wish them a curt 'Good Afternoon' before striding off shaking my head in disbelief. It's interesting to note that very few of those who were involved went on to have long and successful careers in the game. Alcohol has always been an issue in football, but thankfully the availability of recreational drugs is a much more modern phenomenon, although as far back as 1998 one of our young players failed a random FA drugs test at the training ground. There was a school of thought on the board that felt that we should make an example of this young man by terminating his contract forthwith but ever the pragmatist, I made the point that we wouldn't be considering such action in the case of one of our more high profile players. The young man concerned was given another chance although he never quite made the grade at Barnsley Football Club and was released soon afterwards.

If the on the field problems following relegation weren't bad enough, financial pressures at Oakwell were beginning to mount. Our impending relegation would have serious implications on the club's revenues, but a further catastrophe lay in wait. At the beginning of the season the Football League had begun a new television rights contract with ITV Digital, a company formed by Granada TV and Carlton TV. The deal, which had been ratified at the Football League Chairman's Conference at Carden Park Hotel near Chester in June 2000, was worth £315million over three years to the Football League. This was significantly more than the enhanced offer that Sky TV were prepared to make. The net effect on Barnsley Football Club was that as a First Division club we were due to receive approximately £2.7million per year for the three years of the contract. The implication of relegation was that as a Second Division club we could expect at least £2million less per year. All of this became academic when at the end of March 2002 ITV Digital went into administration, meaning the Football League was left without a television contract. The implication was that, overnight, revenue that Football League clubs could had reasonably included in their budgets for the following two years was no longer available to them. The rumours of ITV Digital's financial struggles had been circulating for some time because the viewing figures they achieved had been nowhere near their projections. Nonetheless, all clubs had been led to believe that the contract between the Football League and ITV Digital contained a clause in respect of parent company guarantees – in other words, that if ITV Digital struggled then Carlton and Granada, the shareholders of ITV Digital, would have to meet their liabilities under the terms of the contract. Regrettably, when the situation came to a head, it transpired that not only was such a clause not in the contract, but the full contract had not even been signed. The situation was even more galling because at a meeting of the Football League clubs at Notts County's ground the previous November, the Managing Director of ITV Digital had very publicly assured the assembled clubs of ITV Digital's commitment to the contract. The Football League embarked upon a publicity campaign to put pressure on the major shareholders of ITV Digital – Carlton and Granada – and at the same time began legal action against them in an attempt to claw back the £189million still owing to the Football League under the terms of the deal. This was the first time that a major sports rights contract in the UK had collapsed.

As far back as the previous December the directors, mindful of the financial problems that relegation might bring, authorised Michael Spinks and I to have a preliminary meeting with our bankers NatWest to spell out clearly the implications behind relegation and to request their ongoing support when the situation became clear. That meeting took place in early January 2002, and as Michael and I outlined the forecasts for the various different scenarios that we could possibly be faced with later in the year, it was slightly surprising that our relationship manager seemed unaware of our potential difficulties. However, we were given assurances that we could rely on their support and I left the meeting confident that our strong relationship with the bank over many years would hold us in good stead should we require further support if things went wrong. However, the collapse of ITV Digital completely changed the complexion of the situation. Every club in the Football League was now facing serious financial problems and the confidence in clubs from their bankers vanished overnight. Not only that, the transfer market outside of the Premier League instantly collapsed and so one of the main planks that the board of Barnsley Football Club had expected to form part of our policy to deal with our imminent financial troubles, were we to be relegated, was no longer an option for us. We had assumed that following relegation we would be in a position to sell some of our more valuable assets, and although we managed to move Chris Barker to Cardiff City for a deal worth £600,000, we found it impossible to attract any kind of reasonable interest for other players such as Dyer and Morgan. Our bank requested a further meeting, but rather than offering support to an old and trusted customer who had fallen upon hard times, it was announced at that meeting that from then onwards our account would be handled, not by the normal regional business office in Sheffield, but by the Special Lending Services Department, based in Manchester. Although the name may sound rather innocuous, it will send a shiver down the spine of anyone who has ever dealt with such a section of any bank. Those who run Special Lending Services Departments would argue that their brief is to assist ailing companies through their difficulties, but the reality is that, more often than not, businesses who end up at the tender mercies of these people generally do not survive.

Throughout the 2001-02 season, as the club wrestled with the on and off field problems, interest in investing in the Football Club had been shown from Barnsley-born businessman Patrick Cryne. Patrick was the Chief Executive of leading health software company iSOFT, who had stepped in to become the club's shirt sponsors following the demise of our previous sponsor Big Thing. Patrick's original contact at the club had been Commercial Manager Graham Barlow, and Graham informed me that Patrick had indicated that he could be interested in further involvement with the club beyond his shirt sponsorship. With Michael Spinks present I held a couple of exploratory meetings with Patrick before reporting to the board in that December that he may be interested in investing in the club. It was then formally agreed by the board that I be authorised to officially open discussions with regard to possible investment. Unfortunately, because of the complex ownership arrangements of Barnsley Football Club and the quirky articles of association that governed the club, it made any investment discussions somewhat tortuous. In simple terms, the club was not owned by any one individual. There were approximately 9,500 issued shares in Barnsley Football Club, with our register of shareholders showing that these were in the hands of some 450 separate individuals spread far and wide across the United Kingdom. A further complication was that perhaps twenty per cent of the registered shareholders were uncontactable, which meant that in all likelihood they were deceased. Many of these shareholdings were held in very small lots and in spite of the fact that the directors and their families had acquired a significant number of shares during the latter part of the 1990s in an attempt to block a company called Todwick, which had been specifically formed to acquire shares in Barnsley Football Club by building a significant shareholding in the club and spending considerable sums of money in the process, at no stage did the board have control over more than thirty-six per cent of the shares. Of even greater significance was the fact that the Articles of Association specified that, unlike most normal, modern corporate structures, the voting rights for those shares were limited to 'one shareholder one vote', rather than the more usual 'one share one vote'. On more than one occasion over the years my board and the board of my predecessor, Geoff Buckle, had looked in detail at the possibility of modernising these archaic arrangements, but on every occasion it had been decided that the cost and complexity of doing this, with the strong possibility that the shareholders would reject any proposed changes anyway, suggested that the whole project would have been doomed to failure. The net impact of the ownership structure was that as the chairman of the Board of Directors, I was merely the board's appointee and we all, as directors, were merely grace and favour appointees of the shareholders and could be removed by them at Annual General Meetings or Extraordinary General Meetings. As a point of interest, those same articles specified that no director should receive remuneration for his work, and in my time, it was a rare occasion indeed when any director would receive so much as a nominal sum in expenses. Every director that I have ever known at Barnsley Football Club was happy to provide his services for nothing, always taking great pride in serving the club they loved. Our forefathers who had designed such an ownership structure and who had drafted the company's Articles of Association were clearly wary of the Football Club falling into the hands of one major shareholder, and in times gone by that was a very praiseworthy goal, but in the modern era they merely acted as a disincentive for any individual to invest in the club because it would be unlikely that that individual would easily gain the control that he would have needed to protect his investment. By way of example, my colleagues and I, who had signed personal guarantees during the 1980s, were extremely vulnerable because the shareholders could have removed us from office whilst our guarantees would have remained valid.

The board also explored other funding possibilities, but due to the lack of confidence throughout the financial world in Football League clubs because of the fallout from ITV Digital, we drew a blank. Down the years many people have wondered why no approach was ever made to Paul Sykes, the hugely successful entrepreneur whose success story began in his hometown, Barnsley. I am led to believe that before my time on the board some discussion was held between Paul and my predecessor about the possibility of Paul becoming involved with the Football Club, but those discussions came to nothing. Over the years I spoke to Paul on more than one occasion to see if the situation had changed and he was one of those people who was approached in 2002. Whilst always receiving these approaches in a polite and constructive way, Paul made it clear that he had no interest in investing in football. Other local businesspeople were also sounded out but those enquiries led nowhere.

CHAPTER 14

Administration and Beyond

The summer of 2002 is one I'd rather forget, but sadly the memories of that time will live with me forever. Barnsley Football Club was preparing for life in the third tier of English football for the first time in more than twenty years. That was hard enough to deal with, but nothing like as tough as the financial pressures that were building upon the club. From early in that year the board had met regularly to discuss and act upon the issues that the club faced and cost cutting measures had been put in place. Strenuous efforts were being made to reduce the player wage bill with a number of contracts being terminated by way of a settlement with the player. In spite of all of this it was vital that we remained competitive on the pitch, and it was felt by the manager that with the nucleus of players that we had retained, we ought to be able to bounce back at the first attempt.

Detailed discussions were now underway with Patrick Cryne with a view to Patrick making an investment into the Football Club, whilst the board continued to seek alternative sources of investment. Patrick was keen to ensure that any investment that he made would benefit the Football Club directly and was reluctant to make an offer to the shareholders to purchase their shares. Patrick's view on this matter was perfectly understandable, but the opinion of the board was that, because of the voting structure, he was unlikely to be obtain a majority stake in the club without a firm offer for the shares. The shareholders were, after all, the owners of the Football Club and it seemed to us that it would be a very hard sell to expect the shareholders to vote away their rights without reward. Following a meeting at my home with Patrick on Saturday 18 May, a few days later proposals were received from him in respect of a potential investment into Barnsley Football Club. Those proposals were extremely astute and well thought out but, as expected, did not include an offer to the existing shareholders for their shares. Patrick also requested that each member of the current board would give a written undertaking to support the proposals and to use their best endeavours to ensure that the proposals were successful. At the board meeting held to discuss the submissions, Director Mick Hayselden announced that he, his son Mark, and former Director Mick Hall, were considering forming a consortium with a view to taking control of Barnsley Football Club and injecting fresh capital. Mick further indicated that the consortium would be in a position to make a cash offer to the shareholders for their shares. By early June an outline document was received from the consortium detailing their initial proposals, which did indeed include a proposed cash offer to the shareholders. Both the consortium and Mr Cryne required, as part of their respective proposals, that the company's Articles of Association be changed from the 'one shareholder one vote' system to a 'one share one vote' system. The intervention of the consortium strengthened the board's view that, in all likelihood, the shareholders would reject Mr Cryne's proposals because, even had Mr Hayselden resigned from the board in order to pursue the consortium's interest and we had then been able to have a unanimous board supporting Mr Cryne's proposals, we would have looked pretty foolish at any shareholders' meeting because Mr Hayselden – himself a shareholder – would have simply informed the meeting of his outline proposals. That in turn could have meant a rejection of Mr Cryne's proposals, which the board would have been committed to support. At this stage I need to declare that I and all of my board members and their families each held a relatively sizeable block of shares but I can say, quite categorically, that the prime consideration for all of us was to find a solution to the problems of Barnsley Football Club and that our own personal circumstances were of secondary importance. As the consortium worked up their proposals a request to the board for a period of exclusivity was granted.

All parties were aware of the urgency of the situation, not least our bankers, NatWest, with whom we were in regular contact to keep them informed of progress. Unfortunately, by late August they took the fateful decision to request the directors not to authorise use of our £1million overdraft facility. That sounds as if the board had a choice, but in those situations there is no choice. At that stage we were in credit at the bank on our day to day trading accounts, but with the forecast losses of £2.5million – the amount we should have received from ITV Digital as a First Division club – for that year looming, they clearly decided that supporting one of the great institutions in the town of Barnsley, an organisation that had been a fantastic customer to them over the years, was not worth the risk. Due to this crippling decision, our projections meant that we would run out of money by the end of October, whilst with their continuing support on the overdraft we could have survived until well into the New Year. The only liability that we had to the NatWest group at that time was the business loan on the North Stand, which was around £2.6million and although we were short of cash, we had independent valuations carried out on our assets, which showed that our freehold land and buildings were worth almost £10million. Their decision cranked up the pressure hugely on the board to come up with a solution. On the pitch we had an awful start to the season, with a bad first day defeat away at Swindon and even though results improved slightly, the mood around the club was gloomy.

After a number of meetings with the consortium and their advisors, one of the country's major accountants, Grant Thornton, the board were optimistic that we would eventually arrive at a successful conclusion. However, in early September things finally came to a head in quite dramatic fashion. I had been invited to attend a Supporters' Club meeting, which was to be held at Ardsley House and which, under normal circumstances, I would have looked forward to and enjoyed. I had been a guest of the Supporters' Club on frequent occasions over the years and believe that I had built up a reasonable rapport with the vast majority of fans. That night was a particular difficult one, not just because of the number of fans who were there, some of the difficult questions I had to face, some of the criticism I received, but also because I knew that the consortium was meeting with its advisors at their Manchester offices with a view to finalising their proposals. I felt confident enough to assure the meeting that a solution was in hand and after a long and tiring evening, I prepared to drive home. As I left the car park at Ardsley House, I received a phone call from Mr Hayselden, who delivered the shattering news that the consortium had been unable to agree final terms and conditions for their proposed takeover of Barnsley Football Club, citing the fact that they had been unable to get sufficient bank support for their proposals and had no option but to withdraw their interest. After one more in a long succession of sleepless nights, I gathered the board together for an urgent meeting with the outcome being that, unless a white knight could be found, our advisors made it clear that we had little option but to consider placing the club into administration. I was instructed to contact Patrick Cryne, who was good enough to agree to attend a meeting the following evening at Oakwell. He was appraised of the up to date situation and asked whether he would, at this late stage, consider resurrecting his previous interest in investing in the club. He promised us a response within forty-eight hours and when that came, I was not surprised to learn that he was not in a position to proceed.

A board meeting had been arranged for midday on Saturday 28 September, prior to the home game against Wigan. At that meeting it was formerly decided that we had no option but to seek to place the football club into administration. Matt Dunham, an experienced administrator from accountants Robson Rhodes, was appointed to handle the formalities of seeking an administration order with the likelihood that he and his firm would be appointed by the court to handle the actual administration. For a chairman and a Board of Directors who had for many years been acknowledged in football circles as being financially prudent, this was a shattering experience.

I am proud to say that of the thirteen years in which I presided over the club, we traded profitably for ten of those years. Indeed, such was the reputation of Barnsley Football Club for its sound financial management, I was once asked to share a platform with the then chairman of Watford Football Club, Stuart Timperley, then himself a Professor of Economics at London University, to deliver a seminar to the rest of the league clubs on how it was possible to operate a small town football club successfully on the pitch and be financially viable off it, but having received the invitation, I chose to decline. The decision to seek an administration order was not taken lightly by the board, but in view of projected losses we had little option. In view of the strong asset position of the club, which included a landholding of some thirty-five acres, and the relatively low debt position, the board were optimistic that a swift exit from administration would take place. Administration means, in practical terms, that the responsibility for running the business and finding a buyer for it, passes from the Board of Directors to the administrator. In the case of Barnsley Football Club the administrator was faced with the same problems that the board had to wrestle with. I am sure that many fans will remember those truly horrible times with bucket collections being taken and all manner of fundraising options being supported by our long suffering fans. Within the club, ruthless decisions were being taken by the administrator and his team. Redundancies were made, brutal cost cutting measures were implemented, a loan was sought from the PFA and a number of directors agreed to make a loan of £90,000 collectively to the administrator. The players agreed to a deferral of wages, but in spite of all of this there was the persistent rumour emanating from the administrators that if a speedy conclusion wasn't reached, then the club could fold. Early on in administration it was announced that there had been upwards of forty enquiries, but I felt that it was a mistake to publicise that fact because, as all those experienced in these situations will know, the vast majority of these enquiries melt away like snow in the summer. The attraction to most of those who had enquired was the opportunity to acquire a large tranche of

144

freehold close to the town centre of Barnsley rather than the purchase and running of Barnsley Football Club.

Although the directors no longer had any legal authority over the affairs of the club, we were invited to continue to attend matches and try to engender an air of normality on match days. We were also there to offer advice to the administrator should he require it, but it must be stressed that, contrary to the rumours that swirled around at that time, this was not some cosy cabal where the directors were pulling the strings; the administrator had a legal duty to operate entirely independently, which is what he did. As administration progressed, normal football activities continued, but results continued to disappoint and after seeking the views of the board, Mr Dunham decided to relieve manager Steve Parkin and his assistant Tony Ford of their duties. Glyn Hodges was given the impossible task of managing the first team on a caretaker basis. I'm told in life that it's unhealthy to harbour regrets, but one of mine to this very day surrounds the dismissal of Parkin and Ford. They were both men whom I had come to know and respect enormously in my time as their chairman and I was shocked to learn sometime after their dismissal that, contrary to what I had been told, they would receive no compensation in respect of the termination of their contracts. That situation revolved around the thorny issue of what is known as 'football debt' in insolvency situations. Football debt is seen by the football authorities, but not by the laws of the land, as being paramount and for a club to exit administration successfully, all football debt must be repaid or at the very least there must be a credible plan in place for this debt to be repaid within a reasonable timescale. Bizarrely, football debt consists of unpaid transfer instalments to any club and unpaid or deferred player wages, but it does not apply to managers' or coaches' salaries. I am amazed that this interpretation by the football authorities has never been challenged in law, particularly by Her Majesty's Revenue and Customs who lost their preferred creditor status some time ago.

In spite of the change in the manager's office, results on the pitch continued to be patchy and of particular embarrassment was one night in early November when we went out of the LDV Trophy at Gigg Lane, Bury, with barely a whimper, losing the game 1-0. My anger and frustration boiled over that night in the dressing room where, having had a brief chat with skipper Chris Morgan, I then berated two of the younger members of the team whom I knew were not living their lives properly off the field and whose performances that night had been a disgrace. I even remember suggesting to Morgan that if he felt similarly angry, I personally would have no objection if he took them round the back of the stand to teach them a lesson. In early September we'd already suffered the indignity of going out of the League Cup 4-1 at Macclesfield, thus depriving us of some potential and much needed revenue, but I have to confess that that night at Bury was probably as bad as it ever got. I also lost my cool in September, this time at the McAlpine Stadium, home of our neighbours Huddersfield Town. As I went to my seat I was buttonholed by the agent of Chris Lumsdon, who wanted to talk about a new contract for the player, but given all of the circumstances that was the last thing on my mind. But the guy persisted, informing me that he'd got interest in his player from Preston North End. The agent could not have picked a worse day to promote the interests of his client because, unfortunately, Chris had an absolute stinker that afternoon and I regret to admit that very publicly towards the end of the game, I went across to where the agent was sitting and loudly and rather crudely suggested that perhaps he'd got it wrong and it was Preston Ladies rather than Preston North End that were showing an interest. These two incidents probably reflected the fact that the pressure was getting to me.

Soon after the club had entered administration I was surprised to receive a phone call from the Mayor of Barnsley, Peter Doyle, requesting a meeting. Contrary to perceived wisdom at that time, Peter was not a close friend. In fact, prior to that phone call, I can recall meeting him on only a couple of occasions, the most recent of which had been a couple of years previously when we had both played in a charity cricket match at Stainborough Cricket Club (he claimed my wicket with a medium pace off-cutter). I had assumed that his request for a meeting was in his mayoral capacity and that he wished to

146

acquaint himself with the facts surrounding the demise of one of the town's great institutions. I was further surprised when at the meeting I was introduced to an associate of Peter's, whom it transpired was his financial advisor. I was even more taken aback to realise that the purpose of the meeting was for Peter to pursue an interest in buying Barnsley Football Club. Having acquainted Peter and his advisor with the relevant financial information, he explained that he was keen to save the Football Club and that he hoped that I would help him with that project and that I should stay on as chairman if he was successful. This I agreed to do. Following the meeting, Mr Doyle registered his interest in taking over the club with the administrator Matt Dunham, who by this stage had seen many of those who had previously expressed interest disappear into the night. After much discussion with the administrator, with the Football League and with a group of funders who were to provide some of the finance that Peter required, an offer was eventually made by Mr Doyle to Matt Dunham. The deal with the administrator was completed and by the time we played at Crewe Alexandra on 14 December 2002, Peter Doyle and his family proudly took their places in the visiting directors' box at Gresty Road. There continued to be tortuous negotiations with the Football League, who were not prepared to grant Barnsley Football Club their golden share as a League member, because the route out of administration had not followed Football League regulations. The new regime at Oakwell was not universally welcomed by the fans and some of Mr Doyle's public statements did little to ease the general anxiety felt by supporters about the future of their beloved club. In all fairness to Peter he had tried to do what he could to save the Football Club. For my own part, it soon became clear to me that my position as chairman was merely as a figurehead. Mr Doyle, as was his right, ran things in his own unique way and my only real role was to support and encourage caretaker manager Glyn Hodges as he juggled his resources to try to avoid a consecutive relegation. As the off field turmoil continued, the threat of the drop became ever more real but thankfully, an Isaiah Rankin strike against Brentford on 26 April 2003, secured a 1-0 victory and the three points that were instrumental in preserving our Division

Two status. This horrible season concluded with a 1-0 away defeat at Wigan Athletic who, at that stage, were the runaway champions of the division. From that day onwards, I had almost no involvement with Barnsley Football Club, other than occasional conversations with Glyn Hodges and Michael Spinks to see how they were getting on. My resignation as chairman and as a director was announced on Friday, 20 June 2003, and my nineteen-year stint in the Oakwell boardroom was over.

A question I've been asked endless times over the years is: 'How did we go from a Wembley appearance to administration in the space of two and a half years?' Nobody would be astonished to know that it's a question that has exercised my mind on a regular basis. Simplistically it could be said that the combination of the collapse of ITV Digital and relegation to Division Two within a few weeks of each other meant that we were simply unlucky and that if either of those events had happened individually, as opposed to both of them together, then we would probably have survived. That, however, would be an easy way out because the painful truth is that from the summer of 2000 to the date of administration, the board and I and our various managers made more poor decisions than good ones, whereas in previous years it had been the other way around. I must hasten to add, that as the chairman of the Board of Directors, I was the person ultimately responsible for the affairs of Barnsley Football Club and have never flinched from recognising my own responsibilities. Over the two and a half years of decline our various managers were allowed either to re-sign or bring to Oakwell a succession of players who failed to live up to the task. Many of these men were very highly rewarded – too highly in some cases – but seemed content to simply go through the motions and pick up their money. Another question I've been regularly asked over the years is why did Barnsley Football Club fall into administration when our overall indebtedness, as reported in Robson Rhodes' letter to the creditors in December 2002, was as 'little' as £3.8million whilst other clubs with far higher debt and a smaller asset base managed to survive. The simple fact was that we had run out of money – hard cash – although I have often thought that if our indebtedness to the bank had been substantially higher, then they may have been inclined to have been more supportive. None of this changes what actually happened and I will regret for the rest of my life that my era as chairman ended in such a way and that so many good people were damaged in the fallout from administration.

CHAPTER 15

Over and Out

When I became chairman of Barnsley Football Club in November 1989, English football was at a very low ebb because of the disasters at Bradford, Heysel and Hillsborough and the hooligan problems that had bedevilled the game throughout the 1980s. But from the beginning of the 1990s, football began to rehabilitate itself, the major driver being the formation of the Premier League for season 1992-93. For a number of years prior to that there had been rumours that the First Division clubs were intent upon breaking away from the Football League but it was in early 1991 when, having received the blessing of the FA, they were able to progress this ambitious but very disruptive move. By the summer of 1991 relationships between the First Division clubs and the management committee of the Football League had completely broken down and at a meeting of all clubs at Filbert Street, Leicester on 12 July, the full extent of the breakdown in negotiations was revealed. The First Division clubs simply refused to speak to the elected representatives of the Football League so the rest of us were confronted with a scenario that threatened complete chaos. It was proposed that a group of chairmen from the second, third and fourth divisions be elected in order to liaise with Rick Parry, who was representing the First Division clubs in their negotiations, in order to try and achieve an orderly restructuring of professional football. Myself and the chairmen of Newcastle United, Bristol City, Bury and Lincoln City, together with the managing director of Leyton Orient and well-known and respected former player Frank Clark were elected to represent the Football League's interests on behalf of the management committee. The key issues that we were mandated by the clubs to pursue were the retention of promotion and relegation to the top flight, the continuing involvement of the newly formed Premier League clubs in the Football League's cup competition and financial compensation to the Football League for various revenue streams that may be affected. This was to be my first involvement in the world of football politics and one that I found very instructive, very interesting and thoroughly enjoyable. At the time it was widely believed that the Premier League would go on to be hugely successful, but nobody could have predicted just how great that success would be.

After the formation of the Premier League the image of football began to improve, there was greater commercialisation of the game and there continued to be a flurry of new legislation. All of this and the growth and development of Barnsley Football Club put greater and greater demands on my time as chairman. It became the norm for me to handle transfer and contract negotiations whereas in earlier years the manager would handle such dealings with the chairman and the board merely rubberstamping his recommendations. As the burgeoning influence of football agents increased and contracts became more complex, most clubs took much of the responsibilities away from the manager. In my early years as a director, the majority of contracts were pretty straightforward, consisting principally of a weekly wage and an annual signing on fee. As time passed and agents became more innovative, a whole raft of benefits were being sought. These could range from simple appearance money, goal bonuses for strikers, clean sheet bonuses for goalkeepers, promotion bonuses, league placing bonuses, medical insurance cover, relocation payments, housing allowances, club cars, demands that the client should always remain the highest paid at the Football Club, percentages of any future transfer fee, payments for appearances at international level, image rights as well as clauses that would guarantee the player a transfer should an agreed bid be received. I treated agents as a necessary evil, realising that it was in the club's interest to maintain good relations with as many of them as possible because of their growing influence. There was one situation, however, where things did get rather out of hand. The manager at the time, Dave Bassett, and I had agreed a meeting with one of our academy stars to discuss the offer of a professional contract. We were aware at the time that a particular agent was targeting members of our academy and the agent had made it clear that he was representing the young man in question. It was made very plain to him that whatever advice he might wish to give his client behind the scenes, he was not welcome at the meeting that had been arranged. Nonetheless, he turned up and a very unseemly altercation took place, which resulted in the said agent being escorted from the premises.

For many years surprise has been expressed to me by an awful lot of people that the chairmanship was not a full-time role and I've regularly been asked how I used to manage my time, because not only was my involvement at Oakwell time-consuming, but so were the demands of John Dennis (Barnsley) Ltd. My working day would begin at 4.30am at work on Pontefract Road where I would largely focus on the fruit business until lunchtime. I would try to use my afternoons to commit to the business of Barnsley Football Club, but on days when I wasn't required at Oakwell for meetings with senior staff or outside agencies, I would always speak to the manager and the general manager at least once a day. However, no matter how long I spent at Oakwell I would always go back to my office to tidy up my desk before going home, usually around 7pm. I have to confess that some of my afternoons at the Football Club could not really fall into the category of work because on those occasions I would sit and chat to the various managers and their coaching staff about the issues facing the Football Club in particular and about football in general. It was a joy and a privilege to listen to all of these guys talk of their experiences in football, both at Barnsley and other clubs. It was my working environment that would keep me grounded because many of my customers were very forthright and down to earth people. If ever I had an appearance on one of the early evening news programmes the previous evening, I could be guaranteed to hear the words: 'Saw thee on telly last neet and it put me off mi snap!' The biggest blow to my ego came during a cruise with my family just after we had been relegated from the Premiership. As I was enjoying a cup of tea one afternoon, two elderly couples from Keighley joined me at the table. After a brief chat, one of the men leaned back in his chair and said: "I'm sure I know you from somewhere." I sat there thinking, "*Yorkshire Post, Look North, Match of the Day…*" but after a few moments, he said: "I know where I've seen you… it's in our chip shop in Keighley."

Whilst enjoying good relationships with all my managers, I also realised how important it was to establish good relationship with the supporters. I believe that all Barnsley fans will have realised that I was the same as them – a true Barnsley supporter. I believe, and I may be deluding myself, that I achieved a grudging respect for my efforts, which is probably as good as it gets for any football club chairman. I always tried to make sure that I was accessible to our fans and was always pleased to accept invitations to talk at Supporters' Club meetings as well as regular invitations to speak to Barnsley fans at the likes of Darfield Cricket Club and other venues. Over the years I accepted many invitations to make presentations at various local football clubs and thoroughly enjoyed attending all of these functions as I tried to get across to our fans the message of what we were trying to achieve. I got to know a number of our fans personally and I'm sure two of these will remember a night at Oakwell when our paths first crossed. After a long and tiring day I was sitting in the directors' box watching a turgid reserve match on a cold and foggy night wondering what on earth I was doing there rather than being sat by a warm fire. After about twenty minutes I became aware of a couple of voices from the terrace below making derogatory comments to me. This continued for the whole game so when the final whistle went, I thought to myself that I was going to sort these two out. I dashed down the steps, then down the corridor and confronted the two culprits as they walked off the terrace. They were obviously somewhat taken aback as I invited them into the boardroom for a cup of tea to discuss their gripes. After a thoroughly enjoyable discussion that must have lasted for over an hour, we parted on good terms and to this very day when I bump into them at home matches we always have a chat.

Because of my passion for the club and the tension that I felt on matchdays, I sometimes found it difficult to behave in the restrained and stoical manner that was expected of a director. When you're the chairman of a football club, you understand just how great the impact of what happens on the pitch is to the overall wellbeing of the club with the great frustration coming from the fact that unlike any other business, there is nothing that you can do to influence what's happening on the field. I was never the most relaxed spectator, particularly when things were going badly. Equally, when we scored, I was not always able to restrain myself from showing my joy. Those of us who sat in the West Stand at that time would have been pleased to note that the construction was strong enough to withstand the impact of the large frame of the Barnsley chairman coming back to earth after a very un-chairmanlike leap into the air. After matches, my whole weekend would be governed by what had happened on the Saturday to the point where our friends would discreetly enquire of my wife as to what the result had been and what mood I was in. Many Sundays were spent brooding on what had happened the previous day, but I used to try and avoid speaking to the manager in any great detail either straight after the match or on the Sunday because levels of stress and tension were still very high and, in any event, the manager needed a period of calm before facing another working week. On many occasions my travelling companion and colleague on the board, John Kelly, would join me on visits to a variety of local hostelries in an attempt to either drown our sorrows or celebrate victory. Although John needed no encouragement to be led astray, I do feel the need to apologise to him for the impact my company may have had on his lungs and liver. On one such occasion John and I found ourselves in the Travellers in Birdwell where a group of Barnsley supporters eyed us suspiciously from the tap room. I bought them all a drink and they came round to express their thanks. Inevitably, the conversation turned to the fortunes of the Football Club, which ended with one of them saying: "I've always thought you were a reyt chairman!" My response was: "Yeah, I'll bet you did! You'll have been one of the devils that were shouting 'Dennis Out' last week." And he replied: "How did you know that?" I would also receive regular correspondence from our own supporters, some of whom were serial letter writers. Usually, my own staff at John Dennis (Barnsley) Ltd would assist me in responding, although on occasions I would contact the writer directly to invite them for a meeting to discuss their concerns. Of course, there would be the occasional letters that were simply vile and abusive and they would never receive a response. I also, once, did receive a death threat, which I assumed was from a somewhat distraught Barnsley supporter but, needless to say, whoever wrote it was bright enough not to sign their name.

The privilege of being a director of a Football Club meant that you had access to boardrooms all over the country and it was a lovely experience to arrive at different grounds and be ushered into the private car park and then have access to all parts of the stadium. I was honoured to meet many personalities from public life, not just those from the football world. I was introduced to senior cabinet ministers and other politicians – you always knew when you were talking to a politician because they were the ones looking over your shoulder to see if there was anyone more important in the room – actors, rock stars and television personalities. On one such occasion I didn't really cover myself in glory when, having been welcomed into the boardroom at Huddersfield Town by the Chairman Geoff Headey, myself, John Kelly and his two young sons, Shaun and Chris, were introduced to world renowned actor Patrick Stewart, AKA Jean-Luc Picard. Patrick was a Huddersfield Town fan and was a special guest of Geoff's that day. After our brief introduction Geoff left the four of us with Mr Stewart but unfortunately, not being a Star Trek fan, I didn't really know who he was so to break the ice in the conversation, I asked him what he did for a living. The look of horror on the Kelly boys' faces and the fact that John gently led me by the arm to the corner of the room to explain just who Patrick Stewart really was made me want the earth to swallow me up, but naturally I offered Mr Stewart my profuse apologies. The greatest honour came when, as the chairman of Barnsley Football Club, Christianne and I were invited to a reception at the Metrodome, Barnsley, on 30 May 1991, to mark the official opening of the complex. We were privileged to be introduced to Her Majesty, Queen Elizabeth, and HRH Prince Philip, Duke of Edinburgh. Thankfully, I knew who they were!

One of my hopes on becoming chairman was that the voice of Barnsley Football Club was heard loud and clear in the football corridors of power and I'm pleased to say that over the years our opinions became respected nationwide. On a personal note I used to enjoy the so-called politics of football and was offered the opportunity to stand for election to the Board of Directors of the Football League on more than one occasion, but declined due to the other pressures in my life. In the year 2000 I was pleased to accept a nomination to be a Divisional Representative of the First Division with the additional role of alternate director of the Football League. These roles were much less time-consuming than that of a full-time director but were the reason that Christianne and I were invited to the 'Wembley Final Ball', the last event ever held at the old Wembley Stadium. The function was held in a vast marquee on the sacred Wembley turf and consisted of a gala dinner followed by entertainment provided by, amongst others, Elton John, Jules Holland, Chris de Burgh and Lesley Garrett. One of the more unusual requests for my time came from the Premier League as they fought a legal battle with the Office of Fair Trading (OFT) in a case brought by the OFT under the Restrictive Trade Practices Act of 1976. The OFT were challenging the right of the Premier League to sell their television rights collectively. Barnsley Football Club were believed by the Premier League and its lawyers to be a perfect example of the benefits that collective bargaining brought to the smaller brethren in the Premier League. Having received mountains of paperwork over many months, I was then summoned to the offices of the Premier League's lawyers, a firm called Denton Hall who were based in the Inns of Court, adjacent to the Old Bailey. Myself and the Chairman of Oldham, an old friend, Ian Stott, were both due to appear the following day as witnesses to support the Premier League's case and were briefed extensively until the early hours of the morning on

156

what to expect in court. It was an interesting experience, if not a little nerve-racking, but one that I thoroughly enjoyed.

Over the years, I reflected many times on what I'd said to my father – "If you put yourself up there, you're bound to get shot at" – and I was certainly shot at (figuratively speaking) many, many times. Some of that criticism was justified and some wasn't because unquestionably, mistakes were made and once again I freely acknowledge that as the chairman of the Football Club I was ultimately responsible. On the other side of the coin it would seem logical to assume that perhaps I was responsible for some of the good things that happened as well. Some of the innovations that took place during my time at Oakwell still survive to this day. The Oakwell Centenary Society was born in 1986 and continues to flourish. The legend that is Toby Tyke was born in the early 1990s – and he continues to flourish too. The Study Support Centre has been another great success. Rugby League was played on the hallowed Oakwell turf by both Sheffield Eagles and Wakefield Trinity Wildcats and womens' international football and Under 21 international football both came to Oakwell. During my era three sides of the ground were transformed beyond all recognition, undersoil heating was installed, academy and first class training facilities were developed, a new police control room was built, an electronic scoreboard was added in addition to a brand new facility for our disabled supporters. The car parks behind the East Stand and on Grove Street were landscaped and surfaced and the Reds Superstore came into being as part of the South Stand development. On the playing side, we reached the fifth round of the FA Cup on six occasions and the sixth round on two occasions, we finished one place adrift of the play-offs twice and on a third occasion reached the Play Off Final, when a historic day saw Barnsley Football Club playing in front of the Twin Towers at Wembley for the first and only time in its history and taking part in the last club match at the old Wembley Stadium. Additionally and memorably, pleasurably and unforgettably, there was our promotion season of 1996-97 when Danny Wilson led my beloved Barnsley Football Club into the top flight of English football for the first time in the club's history. And, of course, there was our solitary season in the Premier League where the red shirts of Barnsley competed with the greatest names in football from that era as they graced the Oakwell turf.

So maybe Dennis wasn't such a menace after all...

CHAPTER 16

My Oakwell Dream Team

One of the great frustrations of being the chairman of any football club is that, contrary to popular opinion, the chairman doesn't sit down with the manager to select the team. So, as a little indulgence to myself, and to end on a lighter note, I have picked a team made up of my all-time favourite Barnsley players from my era. The rules are very simple – only those who were at the club during my time as director and chairman are eligible. In going through this exercise, I also came up with a team of players who were rather less successful at Oakwell but my wife told me that it was very undignified and disrespectful. Nonetheless, I'm sure that every fan of Barnsley Football Club over the last thirty years would probably come up with the same names as me.

My goalkeeper would have to be David Watson. A Barnsley lad who gave his all for the Football Club, he was a terrific shotstopper and extremely brave, although perhaps lacking the required height of a goalkeeper in the modern era. David went on to represent England at all levels up to and including the Under 21 age group, and would undoubtedly have had a very long and successful stint in football had a knee injury not prematurely ended his blossoming career. Because of the rules of the game I cannot select my all time favourite Barnsley keeper, Alan Hill, or from the modern era, Heinz Muller, who in his brief Barnsley career was outstanding, but David Watson was still up there with the best of them. Because of my team selection, the system to be played would be three centre-halves with the full-backs pushing on, and for the right-back position, another local hero from the promotion team gets the nod. I refer, of course, to Nicky Eaden, whose Oakwell career came very close to being ended before it had started before Mick Wadsworth and Eric Winstanley advised the board to reverse the decision to release him. Nicky was a great servant to Barnsley Football Club, a solid defender and good going forward. He had the uncanny ability to cross the ball from the most unlikely of angles and was a key component in Danny Wilson's celebrated side. I was always saddened to see Nicky getting stick from the Barnsley fans, even more so when he returned to Oakwell when representing other clubs. Although his Barnsley career was relatively short, the quality, class and experience of Neil Thompson makes him my choice for the left-back position. Neil, of course, is another member of the promotion winning team and his thumping strike early in the season against Stoke City remains one of the highlights of that season. Paul Futcher gets my vote as the third centre-half, or sweeper. Futch was a complex character off the field but a wonderfully talented footballer on it. He wasn't the kind of defender who enjoyed a scrap with a big centre forward, but his ability to read the game and to make time for himself made him a class act. Futch had an excellent career in football, and was one of those who I always felt could have performed at the highest level. My twin centre-halves would be Arjan de Zeeuw and Gerry Taggart, although over the years the likes of Eric Winstanley, Pat Howard, Mick McCarthy, Ian Evans and many others would all have been in contention. Dutchman de Zeeuw, an intelligent and educated man, played an integral part in the promotion season and went on to have a superb career in the Premier League with Wigan Athletic, Portsmouth and Coventry City. Taggart was a beast of a man, hugely talented in many ways. Although he chose football as his profession, as a youngster he had represented Northern Ireland at athletics. Gerry was signed by Mel Machin from Manchester City for £70,000 and he became a cult hero at Oakwell. He wasn't just a larger than life character on the pitch but was just as lively in the dressing room as well. I bumped into Gerry with his pal Brendan O'Connell in the champagne bar at Wembley following the club's defeat to Cardiff City in the FA Cup semi-final recently where to my great amusement he recalled tales of his time at Oakwell, taking the mickey out of me in the process.

My central midfield pairing consists of perhaps two of the greatest players ever to don the red shirt of Barnsley Football Club – captain marvel Neil Redfearn and Ronnie Glavin. There is little more that can be said about Neil Redfearn and his career at Barnsley that hasn't already been said – a fantastic servant to the football club and a great ambassador for the town and a hardworking and goalscoring midfielder who deservedly received the plaudits when he led the team to promotion. That brings me to my old pal Ronnie Glavin, who was in his second spell at Oakwell when I joined the Board of Directors. What a footballer Ronnie was. He was always described in the press as 'the chunky Scot', but he had pace, a great touch and was a brilliant finisher, regularly contributing twenty goals a season. My third midfielder, who would play in the hole behind the front two, would be Craig Hignett. Bright, inventive and talented, in his short career at Barnsley he was simply a joy to watch and his nineteen goals helped Dave Bassett's team to reach the Play-Off Final at Wembley. Up front, in the face of strong opposition, I would have Ashley Ward. Although his career at Barnsley was brief his contribution was immense, particularly during that season in the Premiership when his work rate, strength and ability were an inspiration. Not only does he get selected for what he did on the field, but my chairman's instincts would also dictate that because of the money we made when we sold him, that counts in his favour. Alongside Wardy there's only one choice and that, of course, is Super Johnny Hendrie. A huge influence in the dressing room, John's goals provided the spark that helped us to that famous promotion in 1997. A clever footballer, John provided one of the great memories from the FA Cup run in 1998 with the opener against Manchester United in that famous replay victory.

In selecting this XI, I appreciate that there were other great players who I have overlooked. Goalkeeper Clive Baker, who gave great service to the club; centre-half Larry May, who formed a great partnership in central defence with Paul Futcher; Stuart Gray, a cultured versatile left-footer who could play anywhere down the left and also at centre-half; Stevie Agnew, a quality midfielder and a great passer who chipped in his fair share of goals; Paul Wilkinson, a giant in that promotion season, and David Hirst, who would probably feature as the striker in most fans' picks. Unfortunately, because of his association with that team from Hillsborough, he wasn't eligible for selection for my team. In ending this chapter in the book, I will let the readers decide who my choice of manager of this great squad of players would have been, and as for the chairman of that club, there's no prizes for guessing.